WITHDRAWN

Food Service
Marketing and Promotion

by David D. Seltz

Lebhar-Friedman Books
An Affiliate of Lebhar-Friedman, Inc.
New York

Food Service Marketing and Promotion

Printed in the United States of America
Library of Congress Catalog Card Number: 76–56643
International Standard Book Number: 0–912016–59–0

Contents

Foreword

The restaurant business today is *big* business—the third largest in the country, generating $75.5 billion in 1975. A substantial investment is required to enter this business, even on a small scale. Operating expenses alone constitute a "nut" that grows bigger and bigger every day. Increasing competition adds to this difficulty by dividing your market potential and fragmentizing your customer dollar.

Hence, it's vital to the life of a restaurant that there be constant customer flow to generate the cash flow needed to cover expenses and yield a satisfactory profit. This requires a marketing plan that "thinks ahead," that avoids drift, that insures that you are covering all possible roadblocks. If you fail to do this, your ruthlessly constant fixed and variable expenses can erode both your assets and your options.

To succeed, today's restaurant must:

- attract sufficient patronage on a continuing basis
- be "different"

- achieve a favorable image, both internally and externally
- generate dependable repeat business
- generate favorable word-of-mouth advertising
- understand its varied advertising and promotional needs.

Accomplishing this requires good marketing. It is not a matter of hit-and-miss or happenstance. You must work at it constantly. Take a solid, candid, clinical look at all aspects of the operation: Are you, at this time, reaching the greatest portion of your market place most effectively and economically?

That is the objective of the marketing concepts contained in this book. They tell you what others are doing and what you can do to help make your business distinctive, popular, and profitable. Furthermore, they help to generate the kind of creativity, imagination, and innovation conformant to today's needs; the kind of qualities that may help you cope with competition and assure constant traffic flow.

The ideas in this book may not be universally applicable. Many will apply to you. Others will not. All of them, however, are designed to prod your imagination and to suggest a great variety of creative possibilities that will help you in generating your own ideas.

Chapter 1

Marketing Considerations

DEFINING YOUR MARKET

Let's first consider the meaning of the word *marketing*. It's a term that's often misunderstood, particularly since it's subject to many varied (and often erroneous) interpretations.

Simply speaking, marketing means getting your product (or services) to the market place in the best possible way. By market place we refer to your prospective customers: who they are, where they are, how to best reach them.

Customers—and markets—differ from one restaurant to another simply because restaurants themselves differ so widely. For example, the market for one type of restaurant may be based on motoring accessibility. This is usually the roadside diner that attracts tourists and other mobile, itinerant patronage. Another restaurant's market may be based on price, family convenience, or quick service. This includes the usual fast food chains—hamburger, pizza, pancakes and chicken, etc.—that have sprouted up everywhere. It may also be based on the desire for a specific, specialized type of food.

Ethnic restaurants, varied gourmet restaurants, and steak houses fall into this category. Or it may be based on a unique "style"; for example, a restaurant's entertainment, its distinctive surroundings and decor, its reputation and reflected status. Each of these differentiations creates its own basic market. Each attracts its own selective clientele based on its ability to fill a specific customer need.

IDENTIFYING YOURSELF

To identify your market, you must first identify yourself as you appear to your customers. Take an objective, clinical, across-the-street look at your restaurant. Ask yourself the following questions:

- Exactly what type of customer is attracted to my restaurant?
- Are my prospective customers "everybody?" Do they comprise the entire community, or only specific groups or individuals within it?
- Does my market consist of foot traffic? Auto traffic? Both?
- Is my patronage linked to the location of some nearby traffic-generating enterprise; e.g., a nearby theater, industrial plant, etc.?
- Is my patronage selective, based on my reputation for specialized, innovative cuisine?
- Is my patronage enhanced by an attractive "image?"—the innovativeness of decor, surroundings, entertainment, promotions, etc.?
- Is price a factor?
- Is accessibility a factor?

Initially identifying yourself helps you identify your prospective customers and target yourself precisely to them. This also helps you to achieve:

- greater value for your advertising dollar expenditure, thereby eliminating waste
- an enhanced projection of your specific personality and image among your specific category of customers, thus posi-

tioning you and distinguishing you from other restaurants in your area

● maximum market saturation at minimum cost.

After you have identified yourself, aim to hit your market with the precision of a rifle, rather than the scattering of a shotgun. If, for example, you're aiming at the $12.00-and-up gourmet dinner trade, place your advertising in the specialized pertinent sections of a newspaper or magazine that best reach this particular group. Aiming at the general mass market often results in a serious waste of money and time.

All of these ideas are important to define your market place. To the extent that you pinpoint your market, your prospective patronage, you will achieve maximum exposure and ongoing customer flow. Too many restaurants that aim at *all* markets, willy nilly, frequently end up with no market.

FOUR BASIC MARKET CATEGORIES

Generally speaking, commercial restaurant markets can be grouped into four basic categories. These are:

1. *The Retail Market.* This comprises the fast food or coffee shop type of restaurant. Patronage consists of shoppers, workers, and passers-by in the business areas, students from nearby schools, and others whose dining time, dining budget, and eating desires are basically limited.

2. *The Leisure Market.* This consists primarily of patrons who select their dining facility on the basis of atmosphere, special types of food (usually gourmet varieties), and entertainment offered, rather than on the basis of fast services and accessibility. The leisure market also includes party and special events organizers.

3. *Business/Industry Market.* This is a market that consists primarily of business executives, salesmen, and their prospects and customers. Depending upon the specific conditions involved, this category can include either the retail or the leisure markets. Since these people are often on expense

accounts and use credit cards to entertain customers, they are generally prepared to spend more money for better surroundings.

4. *Hotel and Motel Market.* This market includes customers in all of the above categories. Often, in fact, a hotel or motel will maintain several dining facilities, each one of which is devoted to the specific requirements of each different market.

In addition to its market, restaurants may also be categorized as:

1. *Full Menu Restaurants,* which prepare foods for consumption on the premises.
2. *Limited Menu Restaurants,* which have a specialized, generally fast food type of operation: e.g., pizza, chicken, or hamburgers.

IDENTIFYING YOUR COMPETITION

A famous actor once said, "If you want to learn your part well, learn the parts of all the other players first." The owner of a restaurant could do well to apply this advice to his own business. Who are the other players in your community? And who is your competition? Chances are, you do have competition; most restaurants do. Find out all you can about these competitors. What do they offer? What is their image? Their appeal? Do they offer more for the money than you do? Less? How good is their service? What is their reputation? What percentage of the market have they captured that you believe you should take?

Knowing this information will help you to:

● gauge your status in comparison with others
● guide the marketing direction you take to compete most effectively
● become aware of how your food, price, and service compare with others in your area
● build guidelines for your advertising and promotional approaches.

How can competition affect you? You might be surprised to find that being clustered among many other restaurants is more of an advantage than a disadvantage—particularly if the type of food and atmosphere you feature is positioned differently from others in the area and fills a very specific need. The coffee shop situated among expensive restaurants offers fast food and fast service to budget-minded patronage. And the ethnic or gourmet restaurant provides a welcome change from an overabundance of steak-and-potato places. Conversely, if your restaurant is identical to all the others in the immediate vicinity, and if it appeals to basically the same clientele, you will be at a serious disadvantage.

IDENTIFYING YOUR MARKET THEME

Every restaurant, to succeed, must also have a basic marketing theme. This represents you, your individuality, your reflected image, your points of distinctiveness that will induce customers to seek you out. It's the sum total of the impacts that you convey to your prospective customers.

Such impacts are produced by a variety of qualities, some tangible, others intangible. These include:

A. *Tangible Qualities:*
- your advertising style, media, and message
- your trade name and insignia
- the appearance of your restaurant (both interior and exterior)
- lighting effects, menus, interior signs, etc.
- the quality and distinctiveness of your food, utensils, and packaging.

B. *Intangible Qualities:*
- the quality and warmth of your approach
- the first-impact feeling when one enters your place: Is it comfortable or uncomfortable? Casual or formal?
- the way the customer is seated, served, followed-up
- the uplift to ego and status you give to customers who dine at your place.

Pinpoint your theme. Strive to make it say: "I am different. I offer you more value. I can guarantee you satisfaction and dining pleasure. You can depend on my reliability and on my consistency of quality." This is not expressed in words, but rather in the intangible feeling that a person experiences while dining in your restaurant. It should be the kind of feeling that exceeds adequacy, that instills excitement, and that generates a desire to tell others about your place.

Look around you. You'll notice that practically every restaurant —and, in fact, every other type of business—has a definite marketing theme. This theme may be reflected in the name: "Steak & Brew," "Der Wienerschnitzel," or "Coq au Vin": names denoting and creating an image of a particular food style.

The theme should also be carried out through the uniforms, the menus, the appearance of the place, and the type of service offered. One Chicago restaurant that decided upon a patriotic theme for the Bicentennial made certain that the menus, waitress uniforms, advertisements, and decor carried the red, white, and blue colors, as well as a "Spirit of '76" theme.

These themes and others should be reflected in the style of advertising. This style should tell the reader immediately what the theme of your restaurant is.

The style of an advertisement has several component parts. These include:

- the type style of the ad. Just by glancing at the ad, your customer should be able to recognize the identity of the restaurant
- the general layout and format.
- the headline and copy theme approach.

The proper theme should convey instant recognition, a feeling of the distinctiveness of your place over others, and a feeling of quality food and reliable service. If you are successful, then the sum total of your theme and its impact will generate customer satisfaction and repetitive patronage.

What type of theme should symbolize your restaurant? The following chart put out by the National Restaurant Association contains a Consumer Attitude Survey that provides varied clues to the type of things you should and should not do when structuring a theme for your restaurant.

NRA Consumer Attitude Survey

Reveals Reasons For Eating Out

Rank	Reason	Summary
No. 1	Nobody has to cook or clean up	Importance decreases with age
No. 2	For a change of pace	Most important to $6,000 to $15,000 families
No. 3	For a treat	Most important to 25 to 34 year olds. More important to women than men
No. 4	Good way to celebrate special occasions	Importance increases with age, more important to men than women
No. 5	It's convenient	Most important to persons under 25 and 1 & 2 members in household
No. 6	Going out is a special occasion	Most important to 35 to 44 year olds, importance decreases with income
No. 7	For food not usually available at home	Importance increases with age and income. More important to females
No. 8	It's a good way to relax	Most important to under 25's and persons in upper income brackets
No. 9	The whole family enjoys themselves	Most important to 25 to 34 age group and larger households
No. 10	Spouse requests to eat out	Response provided by males approx. 2½ times more than females
No. 11	Enjoy good food	Importance increases with age
No. 12	It's a good way to entertain guests	Importance increases with age, most important in over $25,000 bracket
No. 13	Restaurant prices are reasonable	25 to 34 age group agreed least with this reason
No. 14	Business requires it	Importance increases with family income and household size, more important to male heads of households

Defines Most Annoying Factors

Rank	Factor	Summary
No. 1	Food quality poor	Most annoying to 25 to 34 age group, annoyance increases with income
No. 2	Poor service	Most annoying to 35 to 44 age group, annoyance increases with income
No. 3	Too expensive	Most annoying to 35 to 44 age group, annoyance decreased with income increases, increases with household size
No. 4	Meals weren't well prepared	Uniformly annoying to most groupings, slightly more irritating to males
No. 5	Poor sanitary conditions	Most annoying to 35 to 44 year old group, more annoying as income increases
No. 6	Eating establishment too crowded	Most annoying to those under 25 and over 55, annoyance decreases with income
No. 7	Too noisy	Most annoying to persons over 45 and in 1 or 2 member households
No. 8	Waiters/Waitresses were rude	Annoyance decreases with age, slightly more annoying to females
No. 9	Portions too small	Most annoying to 25 to 34 year olds, and larger households
No. 10	No place to park	Annoyance increases with age but decreases with income
No. 11	Menus too limited	Annoyance increases with age, decreases with income
No. 12	Didn't have what was on the menu	Uniformly annoying to all segments studied
No. 13	Had to tip	Most annoying to persons over 55, most annoying to lower income groups and females
No. 14	Other people's children are a problem	Uniformly annoying to all groups

SITE SELECTION AS A MARKETING FACTOR

Who are the principal residents? Are they predominantly ethnic groups who seek specific types of foods? Mostly children, who may influence the patronage of your restaurant? Or single apartment dwellers? After you have made your evaluation, aim towards them, not away from them.

Site feasibility is vitally intertwined with marketing feasibility. It is an oft-repeated truism that there are three primary factors contributing to the success of a restaurant: location, location, and location.

This site is more than a physical address, structure, or location. It bespeaks people and constant traffic flow. The site you choose means that you are making yourself accessible to the greatest possible volume of specific categories of people who will patronize your particular restaurant for a specific type of food.

In a recent speech, Verne Winchell, President of Denny's, Inc., stressed the importance of using caution when choosing sites. He advised expansion-happy food operators to "walk before you run," stating that "what is important is the quality of growth. Increasing the number of unit openings each year has become a fashion and is not necessarily indicative of a company's progress." To corroborate this thesis, he pointed out that while Denny's revenues had almost tripled in five years and its net income had increased four times, the number of units in the chain had risen less than 50%.

An in-depth study is required to pinpoint the very best restaurant site possible. This study should consider the following variables:

- Possible changes: traffic patterns, demographics, etc.
- Experiences of previous restaurants: openings and closings
- Current marketing studies relative to the spending pattern of the area. Is it depressed or prosperous? Blue collar or executive? For example, in Connecticut, the industrial city of Bridgeport is considered principally a blue collar area whose residents generally seek the budget-priced restaurant. The city of Hartford, however, with its many insurance companies, is considered a predominantly white-collar area with executives and middle-management people who seek a better type restaurant and are willing to pay more.

- The things you observe while walking down the various streets: What is the general pattern of stores in that city? In that area? Do they conform to your own planned restaurant image?

Successful establishments go to great lengths to decide on a new restaurant site. One Maryland-based chain gathers complete demographic data and customer profiles before they make any decisions. Because they have found that their typical customer has a $10,000 median income level and a better-than-average education, they look for sites in marketing areas in which a minimum of 150,000 people earn this $10,000 median income.

Similarly, the Boston-based Dunkin' Donuts chain has developed a five-year computerized site-selection plan. And McDonald's of Canada carefully studies the basic relationships of a possible location site to both its surrounding area and the firm's marketing objectives.

David Sabo, Executive Vice President of the twenty-six unit Benihana chain, commented that Benihana's primary customer is "a white collar person in the $15,000 to $20,000 income range living within a twenty to thirty minute drive from the restaurant." And, since Benihana specializes in the dinner trade, the chain seeks areas that attract evening patronage, catering particularly to the theater crowd.

Another executive, one who manages the HJ Restauranettes, suggested that you "look at the type of customer that is available in the area. Walk through a clothing store or grocery store. Take a look at the tax rolls in the town hall. See what kind of taxes are paid in the area. Also take a look at other food service establishments in the area to see what their business is like on a Monday afternoon and on a Saturday night. If you can, find out how many restaurants have opened or closed in the area. The Health Department might have records like that. In an urban area you can sell hamburgers by the thousands; in a small town you'll probably want a broader menu so people would be willing to come there more often."

LOCATION CRITERIA

Prime factors that determine potential suitability of location are:

- trading area
- area image

- competition
- zoning and permits
- visibility
- accessibility and parking
- traffic.

TRADING AREA

The area surrounding the proposed site location is your market. Here is where your potential customers conduct their family lives and where you offer them essential products and services to fill their individual and family needs. The volume of business that you do depends largely on the number of people who pass by your doors on any given day.

In a metropolitan area, heavy foot traffic is of paramount importance. This may consist of local residents, transients going to and from work, theaters, or other entertainment centers, shoppers, visitors, and sightseers.

Passing automobiles and other traffic may also be significant, particularly if you provide adequate on- or off-street parking facilities. However, traffic is subordinate to pedestrians. Clearly, too, proximity to public transportation stops or transfer points will encourage patronage. If you are in a suburban area, on the other hand, heavy traffic will be of paramount importance, while pedestrian traffic may be of secondary significance.

In its pamphlet, "Using A Traffic Study To Select A Retail Site," the Small Business Administration lists a number of factors to consider when choosing a site location. (See p. 11.)

"MUST" FACTORS TO CONSIDER
IN SELECTING A LOCATION

In selecting a site for your new restaurant, be wary of real estate developers or brokers who speak of "plans for redeveloping" the area. Also be sure to check out local zoning codes and regulations. Too many times restaurants have gone up and discovered too late that parking was severely limited due to zoning restrictions.

FACTORS TO BE CONSIDERED

Three factors confront an owner-manager in choosing a location: selection of a city; choice of an area or type of location within a city; and identification of a specific site.

If you are going to select a new *city,* naturally you consider the following factors:

- Size of the city's trading area.
- Population and population trends in the trading area.
- Total purchasing power and the distribution of the purchasing power.
- Total retail trade potential for different lines of trade.
- Number, size, and quality of competition.
- Progressiveness of competition.

In choosing an *area or type of location* within a city you evaluate factors such as:

- Customer attraction power of the particular store and the shopping district.
- Quantitative and qualitative nature of competitive stores.
- Availability of access routes to the stores.
- Nature of zoning regulations.
- Direction of the area expansion.
- General appearance of the area.

Pinpointing the *specific site* is, as you know, particularly important. In central and secondary business districts, small stores depend upon the traffic created by large stores. Large stores in turn depend upon attracting customers from the existing flow of traffic. (However, where sales depend upon nearby residents, selecting the trading area is more important than picking the specific site.) Obviously, you want to know about the following factors when choosing a specific site:

- Adequacy and potential of traffic passing the site.
- Ability of the site to intercept traffic en route from one place to another.
- Complementary nature of the adjacent stores.
- Type of goods sold.
- Adequacy of parking.
- Vulnerability of the site to unfriendly competition.
- Cost of the site.

Take a look around before reaching a decision. See how many "For Rent" signs there are. If you see too many, beware.

What kind of traffic flows through the local stores? Are they busy? And does it seem that other businesses are moving in? Or out? Remember: Your store should be located with other successful businesses, since the success of an area will "spill over" into your establishment.

An aura of success should pervade the area in which you are going to locate. This, of course, can take many forms. You may decide to open in the heart of a city shopping or business district, or in a suburban shopping plaza. Wherever you go, be sure you have chosen an "in" location.

Also consider the neighboring businesses in the area. They are of extreme importance. Common sense tells you that certain businesses are good neighbors, while others are detrimental. How would you like to find out—too late—that your business was located next door to a scrap yard?

VISIBILITY

On a city street signs and facades should stand out so that they can be readily seen by the pedestrian as he approaches your site. Corner locations, because they offer maximum visibility, are most desirable, although not always obtainable. Check to be certain that the visibility of your location will not be affected by other projecting signs, marquees, or obstructions in the immediate vicinity. Try to arrange for your signs to be the eye-catchers that are noticed first from the widest approach possible.

On a highway when vehicles are traveling at more than forty miles per hour, the visibility of signs is especially important. Be certain that traffic approaching from any direction will be able to see your signs. Remember that since other traffic, pedestrians, signs, and distractions compete for the driver's attention, you want to make your sign as easy to see as possible.

Chapter 2

On-Premises Promotion

The point of sale for a restaurant is, of course, the premises. From the moment that a person on the street sights your marquee to the time he pays his bill, the equipment and personnel in your restaurant impress him one way or the other and insure that this will be either his first or his last visit.

THE MARQUEE

The marquee is the canopy, the awning-like extrusion at the front entrance of a store. It is the very first of the on-premise tools that attracts attention to your restaurant. It is therefore one of the most valuable promotional means you have, so make good use of it.

First of all, use it to display your name attractively—and legibly. The lettering should be clear and instantly readable. Get a good designer and discuss with him what you need and what kind of display is best: whether you should use neon lights, for example, or painted lettering that illuminates with the proper lighting.

Besides the name of your restaurant, the marquee can be used to announce special events. For instance:

HALLOWE'EN PARTY
Games—Contests—Prizes
Our Food Will Bewitch You!

Or perhaps a business convention is being held in your city:

WELCOME
ELECTRICAL APPLIANCE SALESMEN

Are good patrons of yours celebrating a birthday party?

HAPPY BIRTHDAY
HARRY CALDWELL

Have you persuaded the bridge clubs in the vicinity to hold their yearly tournament in your restaurant?

TOURNAMENT TONIGHT.
BRIDGE CLUBS OF JONES COUNTY

All these announcements may be of local or general interest, and are certainly of special interest to the parties involved. Not only do they increase a warmth of atmosphere, but they also serve to make your restaurant a part of the community.

ATTRACTING THE WINDOW SHOPPER

An attractive marquee is one powerful beckoner. Another is an effective menu in the front window. The menu tells the prospective diner a great deal about the restaurant: the kind of food it offers, the choice of dishes, and the prices. If there is no menu in the window, the customer usually assumes either that the prices are high or that the restaurant caters to a special group other than the potential customer and is not interested in new business. Often, too, he will feel uncomfortable about walking in and asking to see the menu before he has decided to dine there.

Printed menus are generally best, although it is sometimes necessary to have them typed or otherwise processed. The important fact is the readability of the menu. Items must be immediately understandable and arranged in some logical fashion. If possible, leave white space between similar groups of listed dishes. This not only looks better, but it also allows the reader to assimilate the information more easily.

EXTERIORS

The outward appearance of your restaurant tells people what to expect before they ever taste one crisp, perfectly browned French fry. Exterior decorative elements are an attractive force in getting people to come into your restaurant before they know anything about the food. For example, fast food stops along Texas highways aren't much different than they are all over the United States, but a bigger-than-life neon ten-gallon hat or a steer flashing on the roof tells customers that they're part of the Texan larger-than-life mold.

Neon steers might be beyond your budget, however. You can still get a lot of mileage with less dramatic promotion efforts. For example, you can appeal to their gambling instincts with contests. Or you can tell them your restaurant is "their kind of place" by advertising menu specialties in the window.

Start by going across the street and looking at your restaurant from a distance. Is it attractive or distinctive? Maybe it's time for a paint job. Or perhaps some lights need replacing.

OUTDOOR CAFES

While you're critically appraising the restaurant's exterior, consider the possibility of an outdoor cafe. While local zoning laws sometimes restrict cafes, especially in narrow city streets, you'll have to check on those in your particular community. Outdoor cafes are wonderful advertising for you. People almost always take an outdoor table in good weather, which answers one of the first questions that a passer-by will ask: "Is it busy?"

DECOR

Interiors are particularly important, particularly in cities where business generally depends on pedestrian traffic. If your restaurant has large windows, don't block them up or hang heavy curtains across them. They are an invaluable asset, drawing the outside eye to your sun-filled dining room by day and to your candlelit tables by night.

Pile plants in the window. An extremely popular restaurant in San Francisco has raised its many sandwiches to gourmet status by serving them in exquisite inner courtyard, roofed with a skylight and sur-rounded by plants. The fact that the cafe tables are small to allow more people to be seated isn't even noticed by customers who are en-chanted by their surroundings.

Attractive decor travels well; it appeals to people in many differ-ent parts of the country. And if it is done tastefully, a restaurant can redecorate an older building so that it keeps its sense of history but looks modern and spanking new. If there is a fireplace, use it as a cocktail lounge with comfortable armchairs. The fire gives a feeling of intimacy to the whole room.

A successful restaurant can be extremely comfortable without ever being plush, cheerful without being garish. This kind of place started with the 'sixties' "back-to-earth" movement. In fact, the "hip-pies" who grew their own food and ate whole-grain bread have also taught Americans a new element in pleasure: naturalness. And while you can't recreate a charming little forest, you can still artfully sug-gest the blessing of nature by using solid rather than flimsy materials that are real rather than man-made. Don't, for example, paper your walls with imitation wood. Use either real, solid wood paneling or pa-per in a pleasant, low-keyed pattern. This is the kind of feeling that country inns exude.

THE VESTIBULE'S "WELCOME"

Once the diner gets beyond your front door, he enters the vesti-bule. This is where he receives his initial impression of the interior.

Vestibules should convey warmth and welcome. How is this done? Through simple, tasteful, and uncluttered decor. If the cashier's desk is here, it should be accessible, but should not block the passage.

If this is where the diners wait for a seat when the restaurant is crowded or for their party to assemble, it should provide a comfortable place to wait. Benches which can be built along the wall save space and accommodate more people than chairs do.

You might also wish to provide a guest book here in the form of a good-looking, well-bound volume that people can look over and sign while they wait. Or, you might want an easel to place large announcements, such as, "Have you visited our Cocktail Lounge?" or, "Tuesday nights—Cheese and wine tasting supper."

Don't forget the walls. They can carry color photographs or oil paintings of local scenes. This is a good way of adding flavor, interest, and warmth to your restaurant, as well as carrying out the theme of the operation. If you are in the process of opening a new restaurant and have to watch your expenses, try looking into local art schools. In many communities there are excellent painting clubs that may be delighted to display their paintings in your vestibule, a few at a time.

YOUR HOSTESS: A TOUCH OF WARMTH

General Requirements

Your hostess is one of the most vital parts of your operation, since she conveys warmth and dignity. She should give a patron the feeling of being welcomed and wanted. This impression should be conveyed through her appearance, dress, voice, wording, and personality. Good looks are fine, but it is more important that she behave with taste and that she know her responsibility: to offer hospitality and insure the comfort and welfare of the guests.

Age? This, too, is a matter of personality. The important quality to look for is the poise and gentle authority required for hard-to-handle situations.

Knowledge Required

The hostess needs the seating arrangements of the dining room at her fingertips: the complete information about the arrangement of all rooms, whether extra tables have been put in, how many people have called for reservations, and where they will sit. She should seat patrons as quickly and quietly as possible, and, on nights when the vestibule is particularly crowded, she should soothe impatient guests and perhaps suggest drinks at the bar if the wait promises to be a long one.

Public Relations Requirements

An action that never fails to please a patron is to greet him by name, especially if he has a guest with him. A man entertaining an out-of-town friend is very likely to take the friend to a place where he is known and treated as a familiar and valued customer. A good, accurate memory for names is an excellent trait in a hostess: "Good evening, Mr. Blank. Would you like your usual table?"

As patrons leave the restaurant, the hostess should evince care and concern about the food, the service, and/or the general welfare of her customers. If they pass her, she should say, "Good night, Mr. Smith. Did you enjoy your dinner?" "Good night, Mrs. Davis. It was good to see you," or something of the kind. If Mr. Smith or Mrs. Davis stops to praise the meal, she should respond with pleasure: "We're so glad you liked it. Come again soon." She might even suggest that they stop and put this happy thought in writing on the way out on a "Comments Board" if there is one in the vestibule.

If a guest complains, the hostess must take the comments seriously and let the customer know he has been heard. "I'm so sorry," she might say. "We will look into that. Thank you for telling us." While this promise should be made to end the confrontation quickly and unobtrusively, nevertheless she should mean every word. She should check carefully into complaints and inform the management about the slip-ups in service or quality of food that has been brought to her attention. Remember that your hostess is the liaison between you, your dining room employees, and your patrons.

Note: The above applies equally to a maitre d' or head waiter. It is a job where personality counts, whether the individual in charge is male or female.

YOUR AMBIENCE

Now that you have your customers in the dining room, seated at the table, and waiting for their food, what sort of decor meets their eyes as they gaze around? First of all, it should be spotless and orderly.

The paint on the walls should be fresh, and the frames of any paintings or photographs, dust-free.

The type of decor you choose will depend in part on your building. If you are located in an old building, the traditional surroundings —Victorian gas globes and ornate (washable) wall paper, or early American murals and candles on the tables—will blend with your exterior. If you are in a modern concrete and glass building, you will probably want a sleeker, more contemporary style of decoration.

TABLE PROMOTIONS

All sorts of promotional gadgets are available for the tabletop— so many, in fact, that the only caution here is not to clutter the table with too many. "Tried and true" ideas for such items include color postcards with a picture and the address of your restaurant; brochures giving the history of the town or of your own enterprise (these brochures can be simple or elaborate, with or without illustrations, depending on the size of your budget); matchboxes or folders with your restaurant's name, address and telephone number (be sure to order these in a color and lettering that match the rest of your operation); tent cards of miniature billboards. (These serve the same function as an easel in the foyer, but can be more individualized. For instance, instead of "Have You Visited Our Cocktail Lounge?" the small billboard could carry, "For The Bold, The Brave, The Beautiful— Try Our Bloody Mary.")

In deciding which of these aids you want, why not order them one by one in relatively small quantity and keep changing them, featuring some for holiday specials, others for seasonal events, still others for some local event.

TO PAMPER THE PATRON

And now for special ways to pamper your diners and give them something more than just good food and drink: the feeling of being catered to, entertained, and at home in your restaurant.

To pamper the customer you can offer such services as mailing your postcards from the restaurant. This is also an excellent publicity service. Or you might invite them to put their names on your special mailing list to receive announcements of coming events so they will be in time to make the best reservations for, say, a fashion show, an evening of live entertainment, or a New Year's Eve Special. Since you will announce all of these attractions in the local media, you will want to be absolutely sure that your direct mail announcements go out several days early so the recipients will have advance knowledge.

Pampering the customer includes the sound old custom of passing hot biscuits. Is there anyone who doesn't like old-fashioned hot biscuits? Have one of the waitresses take them around the dining room on a large, attractive serving tray or platter. And be sure to be generous with the butter.

WINE ANYONE?

A good way to promote the sale of wine with meals is to have a bottle of appropriate vintage alluringly placed near each table, attractively priced, and offered with a free plate of cheese. This is a very appetizing and "in" combination that few diners can resist.

Do you want your guests to stay longer in the cocktail bar? To linger there until it is time to go on into the dining room and order dinner? Then add a tempting tray of cocktail snacks free to supplement the drinks. These can be assorted antipasto, little sausages, cheese dip, or a wheel of cheese, along with assorted crackers. Try offering more than just a dish of peanuts and see what happens. Since you will hopefully get return customers, change the hors d'oeuvres at least several times a week. Challenge your chef's ingenuity in varying these snacks.

BARS

Bars are still big gathering places where people can get together informally. This is also the area where you have your greatest markup. Encourage people to come into the bar by hanging up a dart board or by putting a small billiard table in the rear. Players will hang around for hours waiting for their turn.

Gather people into the bar through a "Get Acquainted" day, sometime in the spring, perhaps. With the increasing number of meeting places for single adults, bars have become an acceptable meeting spot—and one of the most lucrative aspects of a restaurant's business. I know one restaurant in New York that has literally kept itself alive through its bar, complete with bands on certain nights of the week.

Whether you wish to court your single patrons or not, you can serve cheese and crackers or more elaborate hors d'oeuvres, advertising your offering with a sign in your window. One Cleveland restaurant asked faithful customers to write down on a piece of paper why they liked the place. They photographed their comments, put them all on a poster, and put the endorsements in the window.

You might also feature a special drink concocted by your bartender. Bars in San Francisco, for example, are known for their Irish coffee; some places even use a variety of liqueurs in addition to Irish wiskey.

To increase their early evening trade, many bars offer a "Happy Hour," with special prices below those of the dinnertime and late evening hours. Or they serve two drinks for the price of one and a half. You can think up a lot of variations on this to begin the cocktail hour earlier and to end it later.

If you want a warm and cozy atmosphere, add a touch of the English pub: Install a rack for newspapers and paperback books. Customers can add to your collections by dropping off books they've finished. And if your bar does a large tourist trade, package ready-to-mail souvenir items. You might even put up a bulletin board for local meeting notices, sale items, apartments for rent, and other local news announcements. Make your bar the "in" neighborhood meeting place.

WHAT ABOUT THE SMALL FRY?

People appreciate any attention you give their children. How about offering "children's portions" at a lower price? Since children don't eat as much as adults and often push the food away, why not offer smaller portions at a smaller price? You might even decide to publicize it as a "Family Night," when a child's meal costs half the usual price.

On family days like Thanksgiving or Christmas, you might also give out inexpensive toys to keep the younger set happy. You can heighten the fun by letting them pull the toys out of a colorfully decorated grab bag or previously advertised Children's Treasure Chest. A child doesn't care whether the toy he receives is plastic and highly

PROMOTIONS

The Goodman Theater Offers Its Patrons A Fabulous Meal Ticket At Chicago's Famous Downtown Blackhawk Restaurant

Enjoy a pre-theater prime steak or fresh seafood dinner at a special price—and park your car for one dollar all evening (except Sunday).

No need to rush dinner to make curtain time . . . just call 726-0100 for your reservation at the Blackhawk, Wabash and Randolph (just a few short blocks from the theater) and say you're going to the Goodman.

A fine dinner and an excellent play . . . a perfect combination for an evening of entertainment . . . and don't forget—one dollar parking.

Dinner from 5 p.m. daily. Sundays from 4 p.m.

don roth's blackhawk
726-0100
WABASH AT RANDOLPH

American Express cards honored.

Take our "Brunch Bus" to the Bears games... It's a winner!

For just $5.50 you get a combination that can't be beat:

- All-you-can-eat delicious buffet brunch
- Round-trip bus service to Soldier's Field
- Complimentary cocktail after the game
- $1 dinners for your children under 12 on any Sunday during the season.

Sumptuous buffet brunch every Sunday for $4.25 from 10:30 a.m.

Reservations a must! Call 537-5800.

DON ROTH'S "A Blackhawk Restaurant"

IN WHEELING
On Milwaukee Avenue—North of Dundee Road

Take the carefree way to the Lyric and the Symphony, theater and sporting events, too!

The "Show Shuttle" is our complimentary round-trip bus service for our dinner guests.

Park just a few steps from our door, all evening for $1.

And enjoy the primest of prime beef and the freshest of fresh fish.

Be sure to make reservations. Call 726-0100.

don roth's blackhawk
Wabash at Randolph

Chicago's Don Roth's Blackhawk restaurant promotes a number of events and special tie-in dinners.

As a tie-in with Rochester Red Wing Baseball games, this "table tent" offers a dinner for two when you buy a book of 10 baseball game tickets.

ROCHESTER Red Wings

BASEBALL & DINNER
"A Great Combination"

RED WING BOOK TICKETS (Ten General Admission) are on Sale. With the purchase of one (1) Book at $15.00 ($17.50 Value) you will be entitled to a Dinner for two (2) at CARL ARENA'S TOP OF THE PLAZA. Ask your waitress for details.

MIDTOWN TOWER HOTEL
546-2490

don roth's blackhawk
on pearson presents

jungle vignettes
by gustavo novoa

Chilean-born Gustavo Novoa is known internationally for his beautifully painted fantasies of jungle life. His paintings are in important collections in Europe, South America and the United States. He is represented exclusively throughout the world by Wally Findlay Galleries International.

Wally Findlay Galleries
On "Little Michigan Avenue" just west of the Water Tower
New York, Paris, Chicago, Palm Beach, Beverly Hills

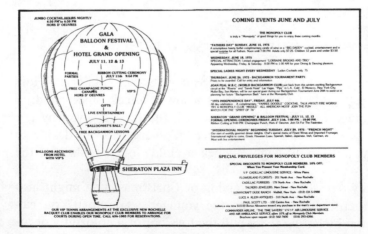

The Sheraton Plaza Inn in New Rochelle, N.Y., promotes its "Monopoly Club" and activities.

Come to our
Mexican Festival
Enjoy any
SAUZA TEQUILA
drink for only **99¢**

Join the señors & señoritas
Nell Gwyn's Taverne
this Wednesday
4 p.m. till closing
Park Avenue
and 42nd Street

BRING A FRIEND TO THE FESTIVAL

FREE GIFTS
BRING THIS NOTICE AND BE ELIGIBLE FOR SURPRISE FREE GIFTS FROM UNDER THE SOMBRERO

NAME
ADDRESS
(PLEASE PRINT)

"Mexican Festival" promotion
by Nell Gwyn's Taverne.

Mel Markon's
2150 N. LINCOLN PARK WEST   525-5550

SECOND ANNUAL THANKS
for your patronage
and your helpful comments.
In appreciation, here's
our gift to you:

For the month of
October only
Two Lunches
for the price of
One

If any two of you order any of our luncheon
entrees or soup and sandwich special,
you get the lesser priced luncheon free.
(Beverage not included)

**CLIP THIS COUPON AND GIVE IT
TO YOUR WAITRESS
WHEN ORDERING**

MEL MARKON says THANKS

Order two lunches,
get one of them free
(Luncheon entrees or
soup-and-sandwich special)
(Beverage not included)
Good any Monday thru Friday
11:00 am   4 pm
Offer good Oct 1-31, 1975

As an annual "thanks" for patronage, Mel Markon in Chicago offers two lunches for the price of one.

Weekly newspaper columns dramatize New York's White Turkey restaurants' meals and other happenings.

THE WHITE TURKEY RESTAURANTS
12 E. 49th St. off FIFTH Ave. 421-6164
MADISON Ave. at 39th St. 685-1710
Open 7 days

Now In New York
TV Superstar Visits Midtown

One of the true milestones on television has got to be Wonderama. It's been on every Sunday morning, from 8 AM to 11 AM, on Channel 5, for as long as I can remember. Kids absolutely adore the program. And you can rest assured that the management of the recently re-opened Autopub Restaurant is aware of the smashing success of this unique TV program, too. So arrangements have been made for *Bob McAllister* — Wonderama's delightful host — to make two special appearances at the 59th Street and Fifth Avenue restaurant tomorrow and next Saturday — March 20th & 27th. Leave it to the Autopub to re-open with a bang! Bob'll be available to sign autographs for and chat with his legion of little fans, and to show them around the Autopub — the only vintage automobile museum in the city!

Incidentally, Sundays are special days at the 'Pub, too, 'cause that's when the luscious Sunday Bubbly Brunch is served. Think about the elegance of non-stop Champagne & Orange Juice cocktails (you keep drinking . . . the waiters keep pouring!), a magnificent platter loaded with a posh assortment of grilled meats, a complementation of the most au courant New Yorkers, and you've got the picture of Sunday Brunch at the Autopub!

As we get closer and closer to the very social Spring months, the invitations to graduation parties, retirement parties, Sweet Sixteens, Bar Mitzvahs, confirmations, weddings, anniversaries, etc., etc., etc., are beginning to flood the mails. If you're an inviter, as opposed to an invitee, then stop biting your fingernails and calm down. Mr. Dave Rubin was born to save you from the misery of party-giving. Dave is the dynamo behind *Party Line* — a one phone-call organization that does everything for the host and/or hostess except mail 'out the invitations. Party Line books the room (based on your personal guidelines), guides you in selecting a menu, arranges for music and entertainment if you wish, parking, and all other essentials. Does it make any sense for you to be hassled when Dave can take care of everything? And at no extra cost to you, either! Party Line's number is 563-7450.

BULLETIN: The White Turkey Restaurant, scene of nostalgic dinners in the true American tradition, is now in Rockefeller Center. Now there's classic dining for smart Fifth Avenue shoppers, Rockefeller Center visitors, St. Patrick's worshippers (the White Turkey serves a sensational Sunday brunch) for convenient lunches or dinners, 7 days a week. The new midtown address is East 49th Street.

The name *Bill Boggs* has always been well known and well respected among professional newspeople — even before he took over the helm of Metromedia's *Midday Live* show seen here on Channel 5. But when Bill scored the first televised in-depth interview with *Frank Sinatra* a short while ago, his name became a household word around the country. Recognizing this extraordinary journalistic feat, Luchow's Restaurant will honor Bill Bogg's this Sunday evening at their *Sunday Celebrity Salute.*

Bill and Luchow's have always been dear friends; Bill swears the only Roast Goose worth eating in this city is the crisp bird that Luchow's fills so abundantly with Apple and Raisin stuffing and garnishes with the most delectable Chestnut Puree ever! As Bill tells it, he has, only on the rarest of occasions, left a slice or two of roast goose to be taken home in a "doggie bag." (No one ever leaves anything at the restaurant. If it's left over, the staff gladly packs it up for your home refrigerator.) But the one thing he never leaves the tiniest morsel over of is Luchow's divine Lingonberry Pancake. And don't I know what dear Bill means! The stuff is addicting! What with fresh, plump, deliciously sweet lingonberries back in season, I drool at the very thought of Luchow's lingonberry pancakes, flambeed right at the tableside, as the finish-touch to end a perfect meal.

New York City's smart young singles crowd seems to have moved, en masse, from their First Avenue hangouts to The Crowing Cock bar and restaurant nestled in the Hotel Roosevelt on 45th Street and Vanderbilt Avenue. Lots of plush sex draws them — the super piano playing of Earl Palmer, the cozy little corners where intimate conversations are shared, the free hot hors d'oeuvres, bartender Paul's generous pourings and, of course, the lively, vital and sensational looking crowd of liberated men and women who know how to live each day with gusto!

by Ellen R. Grimes
Address: Nat'l Press Bldg
97 W. 54th St.,
New York, N.Y. 1001

Almost every night offers a special event of some kind at Sage's East in Chicago.

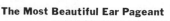

The Most Beautiful Ear Pageant

*an earatic spoof of beauty contests. done with tongue in ear.
You ear invited to attend and also to parteareicipate.*

AWARDS
Winners will receive mink ear muffs.
and a free eye. ear. nose & throat check up.

REARFRESHMENTS
Ear (of corn) & Beer

Sage's EAST
192 EAST LAKE SHORE DRIVE
WHITEHALL 4-1557

THE PEOPLE AT SAGE'S EAST are searching for the most beauteous male and female ears in Chicago. Anyone may enter. There will be a Grand March

EARREGULATIONS

You will be .
You will pas
except your
order that th
cartilage. s
charactearics

One winning

• Winner wi
• They will
• They will
• Just one .
• They will
• This conti

Sage's EAST

HOROSCOPE

Societe Au Gourmet Extraordinaire

presents

A MOST ELABORATE PICNIC

served in the grand manner with a menu from the French Countryside

FRIDAY, JULY 23
6:30 p.m.

Sage's EAST

FEBRUARY IS

Washington's month

AT
Sage's EAST

in the Lake Shore Drive Hotel
181 EAST LAKE SHORE DRIVE
WHITEHALL 4-1557

breakable. What he loves is the glamour, mystery, bright colors, and attention he gets with everyone watching as he draws the prize.

Children's birthday cakes, complete with the child's name on the cake, are worth the trouble they take to prepare because of the pay-off in parent good will. Encourage your patrons to let you know when their children's birthdays come up; you may find your customers making a yearly tradition of celebrating in your restaurant. If you have the time, you might even find it worthwhile to keep a file of customers' birth dates.

PATRON PREFERENCES: WATCH THEM

Guest Files

Birthday celebrations need not be confined to children. Adults like to be fussed over, too. This is one reason for compiling a Guest History File that includes each customer's name, address, and telephone number (business and residence), birthday, anniversary, and other significant dates or facts you may learn of. You should also note whether this customer has ever held a party, large or small, in your restaurant, and if so, when. Remember that everyone likes to have small preferences remembered and catered to.

Use Customers in Your Advertising

Another way to promote your restaurant and at the same time let your best patrons know you value them is to ask if you may quote them in one of your ads: "What John Smith Thinks of Blue Ribbon Restaurant: 'Best Food and Service in the County!' "

Or, you might offer a "chatty personalities item" to the newspaper, like, "Seen at table for two in the Blue Ribbon's Cocktail Lounge, Joe Bailey and Susan Carson, Jim and Julie Ferguson, and the newly engaged Liz Ferris and Tom Kelly." When this comes out in print, send a clipping to each of the people mentioned, with your card.

FAMILY NIGHT

Family night dinners, with special prices and carefully thought-out menus, are always a good feature. Here is where those children's plates can be combined with the regular dinner to make a package price.

Who is the guest of honor? If your advertising has been urging, "Give Mom a rest," make sure she is the center of attention; a gift to each "Mom" is a gracious gesture—a small box of chocolates or a rose—if you can make the right deal with your local supplier.

SPECIAL NIGHTS: GO INTERNATIONAL

Your restaurant business can often be increased when you feature special nights, such as "Hawaiian Night," a smorgasbord "Night In Sweden," a "New England Night," featuring brown bread, baked beans, cod, and maple syrup on the ice cream, and so on. Fit the decor and the menu to the kind of night you are featuring. This does not necessarily require an all-Hawaiian menu, for example; you can offer just one or two Island specialties, along with a lei for each guest. If you can hire a Hawaiian steel guitar player, so much the better. If you can't, get a recording. The atmosphere is the thing.

And how about one or more International Rooms as part of your operation? An English Pub Room, an Italian Room, or a Mexican Room can add interest and a change of pace. With a minimum of expense but considerable effort and imagination, you can offer a real change of atmosphere from one room to the other. In the English Pub Room, you can offer ale in mugs, roast beef specialities, plum pudding, steak and kidney pie. Antlers on the wall and recordings of English music hall songs can complete the ambience. For the Italian Room, you might put candles in Chianti bottles, use checkered tablecloths, and offer Italian specialties and Italian wines on the menu.

REGULAR HOLIDAYS

Religious Holidays

Then there are the regular holidays that come up almost every month. Keep a yearly chart like the following, noting the dates of all holidays. Your chart will show you the holidays you get extra business as well as those you get less business. For example, if you have a considerable number of Jewish patrons, they will not be dining out on Yom Kippur. Ash Wednesday, Holy Week, and Good Friday are not

HOLIDAY	1977	1978	1979
New Years	Sat. Jan. 1	Sun. Jan. 1	Mon. Jan. 1
Lincoln's Birthday	Sat. Feb. 12	Sun. Feb. 12	Mon. Feb. 12
St. Valentine's	Mon. Feb. 14	Tues.Feb. 14	Wed. Feb. 14
Ash Wednesday	Wed. Feb. 23	Wed. Feb. 8	Sat. Feb. 24
Washington's Birth.	Mon. Feb. 21	Mon. Feb. 20	Mon. Feb. 19
St. Patrick's	Thur.Mar. 17	Fri. Mar. 17	Sun. Mar. 17
Palm Sunday	Sun. Apr. 3	Sun. Mar. 19	Sun. Apr. 8
Good Friday	Fri. Apr. 8	Fri. Mar. 24	Fri. Apr. 13
Passover	Sun. Apr. 3	Sat. Apr. 22	Thur.Apr. 12
Easter Sunday	Sun. Apr. 10	Sun. Mar. 26	Sun. Apr. 15
Mother's Day	Sun. May 8	Sun. May 14	Sun. May 13
Armed Forces Day	Sat. May 21	Sat. May 20	Sat. May 19
Memorial Day	Mon. May 30	Mon. May 29	Mon. May 28
Flag Day	Tues.June 14	Wed. June 14	Thur.June 14
Father's Day	Sun. June 9	Sun. June 18	Sun. June 17
Independence Day	Mon. July 4	Tues.July 4	Wed.July 4
Labor Day	Mon. Sept. 5	Mon. Sept. 4	Mon.Sept.3
Jewish New Year	Tues.Sept.13	Mon. Oct. 2	Sat. Sept.22
Yom Kippur	Thur.Sept.22	Wed. Oct. 11	Mon. Oct. 1
Columbus Day	Mon. Oct. 10	Mon. Oct. 9	Mon. Oct. 8
Veterans Day	Mon. Oct. 24	Mon. Oct. 23	Mon. Oct. 22
Hallow'een	Mon. Oct. 31	Tues.Oct. 31	Wed. Oct. 31
Election Day	Tues.Nov. 8	Tues.Nov. 7	Tues. Nov. 6
Thanksgiving	Thur.Nov. 24	Thur.Nov. 23	Thur.Nov.22
Christmas	Sun. Dec. 25	Mon. Dec. 25	Tues.Dec.25

times of festivity, although since many people still avoid red meat on church fast days, sea food should be prominent on your menus during the Lenten season.

National and General Holidays

But there are plenty of holidays you can exploit as feast days. On Christmas, Thanksgiving, and Easter, you will want to emphasize the family element. Why not try hiding eggs for kids on Easter? On Mother's Day you will flatter . . . guess who. On St. Valentine's Day you can attract the young people, perhaps with live entertainment and a gift for the most recent newly-weds. Hallowe'en is a day you can have special holiday costumes for the waitresses, a jack-o'-lantern on each table for candle light, and a tub of apples for bobbing. On the Glorious Fourth, go red, white, and blue; for St. Patrick's Day, go green. There are local anniversaries, too, and state anniversaries, like San Jacinto Day in Texas.

In fact, you might even consider organizing a holiday special on the anniversary of your restaurant's opening: "October 5: Blue Ribbon Restaurant marks five years of giving dining pleasure to our friends. Come one, come all, and join the fun! Special menus, special entertainment, special prices. And the V.I.P. service you always get at the Blue Ribbon." Feature such publicity as this, along with special prices for parties.

All these items must be planned weeks ahead, of course: announcing and advertising the day in the press and on local radio and television stations, printing the menus and getting any extra help necessary, organizing the decorations and favors, and arranging for the entertainment.

LIVE ENTERTAINMENT

Live entertainment, either on special occasions or on regular Saturday nights, can be very profitable. Entertainment tends to increase sales at the bar and helps build business in the dining room. If it's live, the entertainment also enables you to charge more on the days it is offered. However, it is expensive and requires considerable thought if you are to choose the right kind for your particular establishment. Be sure that the entertainment you hire is appropriate for your place and for your patrons. Once you are sure and arrange for it, let everyone for miles around know about it in advance.

AUDIENCE PARTICIPATION

Audience participation in live entertainment like sing-alongs are usually enormously popular. Square dancing can also go over well in some localities. Many communities even have square dance clubs and groups. You might contact the ones nearest you and arrange a Saturday night square dance in one of your rooms, or, weather permitting, outdoors.

Publicize the event in local papers. Prepare small handbills. Ask local merchants to display the handbills, and posters, too, if you decide to print some. Some of the square dance buffs might even help make some posters, or at least spread the word around the neighborhood. Consult with the dancers and get the best caller possible. If such a dance brings in enough business, you might decide to make it a regular feature of your establishment.

TAKE-OUT COUNTER

Have you thought of building your business by adding a take-out counter or department? If so, it should be situated so that the patrons see it as they approach the vestibule on their way out. Here you can display cakes and confections—specialties of the house that are made on the premises—with emphasis on seasonal goodies like fruitcakes and appropriately boxed candy for Christmas, candy eggs for Easter, (special order) birthday cakes, homemade bread, or fresh doughnuts temptingly displayed.

While this kind of project calls for an able, imaginative, and well-paid chef, it can add to profits and even develop into a mail order department in time. Word of mouth is your best advertising here, although newspaper and local magazine publicity helps. Invite the food editors to come in and sample the food on opening day, and thereafter whenever a new speciality is brought out. This is also a good place to offer gift certificates for meals and for cakes, pies, or candy.

When the diner leaves your premises with one of your delicacies, he will be reminded of your restaurant every time he eats a piece of the cake or pie, soothes his nerves with one of your goodies, or feels healthy eating your all-natural bread.

Thus you will aim to make your restaurant a haven for relaxation and culinary enjoyment for your patrons. When they are off-premises, you should try to remind them of your restaurant's attributes through advertising, through news items in the local paper, through word of mouth, and through a take-home reminder from the take-out counter.

PACKAGING FOR TAKE-OUT ORDERS

Attractive and even distinctive packaging of take-out orders is important for two reasons: 1) It pleases your customers, and 2) It attracts new ones. Look into the possibility of an unusual design or your name imprinted on your paper cups, plates, and wrappings.

CATERING SERVICE

Increase your business without increasing your rent with a catering service. Invent intriguing new fillings for sandwiches. Or, try a gimmick like the once very popular six-foot hero sandwich. If you have the space, you might want to stock a few carefully chosen party accessories such as matching plastic plates, cups, forks, and paper tablecloths. Advertise the one-stop convenience of your catering service for busy party-throwers. You might even want to hire people to hand out flyers announcing your doorstop service. In spring and summer, this service can become a picnic center with baskets and other easy-to-carry supplies.

Promote your catering service by getting to know custodians and people in charge of hiring auditoriums. They are often asked to recommend caterers. Maintain a list of important affairs held by clubs, businesses, and civic groups. Call them well in advance of their annual events and suggest your restaurant or catering service.

Also send stickers to switchboard operators at nearby firms. The stickers should be small, giving only your name and address. These can be used for immediate reference in case the operator is asked to recommend a take-out place for breakfast or lunch, or for a place to eat by someone from out of town.

Try to bring your take-out service to employees as well. Ask the managers of nearby commercial buildings if you can wheel a truck through the building at morning and afternoon coffee break times. It should have a bell to announce your arrival at the door of each firm.

Chapter 3

Establishing Your Image

It happens in every community. You see two stores. They sell the same merchandise and charge the same prices. They seem as similar as two peas in a pod. But one store is empty, while the other, full. Only one is prospering and crowded with customers. How do we account for the difference in business?

It's not really that much of a mystery. Generally speaking, the difference between the winners and the losers can be attributed to one word: *image*. And while the word itself is simple, its meaning is not.

Image is essentially the collective impression of everything associated with your restaurant created in the mind of the public, from how you look to what you say about yourself. Very simply, the successful enterprise has an image that appeals to customers and stimulates their patronage. The unsuccessful one does not. The kind of image that you create helps to bring a prospective customer into your restaurant instead of into your competitor's. It means eager, constant, repeat business rather than casual, occasional sales.

Everything you do to attract customers within your particular market results from, and has an impact on, your image. *Image* is a highly complex idea and involves an infinite variety of factors. It is also all-important to your restaurant, as it is to all types of businesses. It is one of the items that persuades prospects to try you and, once they know you, to give you repeat business.

It is your image that prompts a customer to select your restaurant above your competition and to go out of his way to patronize you. And your image results in the most effective and least expensive form of advertising—word of mouth—whereby a customer tells a friend, "I've found the most wonderful place to eat." Conversely, a poor image can destroy a restaurant's business almost overnight.

YOUR ESTABLISHMENT'S OUTSIDE APPEARANCE

Is the entrance to your restaurant appealing? Does it adequately represent the style and quality of the food you offer, as well as the comfort and luxury of your seating facilities? And does it, in some way, indicate the general price range of your meals? Remember that while you may want to convey comfort, you will be limiting your market if your exterior seems to shout, "Come in at your own risk."

Be aware that the outside of your store comprises your facade. It is the first impression that your prospective customers receive. Whatever signs or other accoutrements he sees when approaching and entering your establishment should reflect your establishment and present you at your best.

INSIDE APPEARANCE

Developing a prospect's image of you becomes critical once he is inside. The first impact he receives upon entering should convey a sense of a) warmth at being greeted and recognized quickly, b) good management, due to the neat, organized, and orderly seating arrangements and general overall appearance, c) comfort and, in some cases, luxury, and d) most important, consideration for the customer as an individual. The customer should be made to feel important upon his entrance to your establishment. He wants to feel appreciated and even esteemed for having selected your restaurant from among all others.

PERSON-TO-PERSON IMPACTS

As every restaurant customer can attest, restaurant employees—waiters, waitresses, cashiers, and even kitchen help—play a vital role in establishing its image. An inconsiderate or incompetent waitress, a brusque or unsmiling cashier, and even brash or unpleasant busboys all are identified with the restaurant's management. In the customer's eyes they represent a restaurant that is also inconsiderate, incompetent, or uncaring. Almost always, the individual failure of the employee becomes projected on to the entire restaurant. There is no excuse for ill-mannered or incompetent help. Pleasant, efficient workers are an absolute "must."

ADDITIONAL IMAGE BUILDERS

Printed materials, menus, signs, and other informative literature which is either placed upon tables or passed out to customers also has a definite effect in creating an image. In planning such items, you should make sure that they convey careful thought and selectivity. They deserve your ungrudging time and effort.

IMAGE FORMERS: STRUCTURE AND DECOR: REAL-LIFE EXAMPLES

Both the outer structure and the inner decor are important in enhancing a restaurant's image. Both must be attractive, pleasing, and in good taste. Both must blend in with the restaurant's personality and food style.

Der Wienerschnitzel's "Concept 80" restaurants, symbolizing the look of the '80's, offers many innovations, including a modified A-frame design, landscaping around the buildings, and decor that reflects the mode of each particular marketing area. For example, one unit near the California Angels' baseball stadium in Aneheim, California, has a baseball motif.

Blackhawk Restaurant in Chicago once displayed the art of some outstanding American artists. These paintings were borrowed from the Nancy Lurie Gallery.

Jonathan Livingston Seafood in Westchester hired a designer to enhance its image. His innovations include a feeling of gentle waves, achieved by undulating mirrors and booth curvatures, simulated walls, and partitions.

Ponderosa attains its image through personal services. A server goes to each table to give free coffee, as well as to help parents with children. When it rains, someone is sure to meet customers at their cars with an umbrella.

A&W Rootbeer has upped its profits considerably through changing its image. It now has a dining room with nostalgic items such as Tiffany lamps. There are also fireplaces and replicas of locomotives and river steamboats. The decor combines both attractive design and color coordination. In fact, since they have instituted a new image among their restaurants, sales have risen dramatically.

In his decor, the *Hardee* franchisee in Ames, Iowa, uses a colorful steam locomotive train that extends the full length of one room. The train has four cars and a caboose, each seating up to six people. One car is decorated with a western motif. Another with pennants and the orange and black colors of nearby Ames High School. People can return to the same restaurant and dine in a different setting on successive days.

Nostalgia keynotes *Houlihan's Old Place* in Kansas City. This includes such items as church pews, old clocks and appliances, Tiffany lamps, stained windows, a barber pole, and a ship's figurehead. Even the waitresses carry out this motif, with their old-fashioned long skirts and quilted tops.

The Brothers Two Restaurant and Pub in Atlanta decorated its walls with feature ads from the various advertising and promotional agencies in the city. In addition to an interesting decor, this encourages patronage from various ad agencies.

Among the items in the decor of the *Forum of the Twelve Caesars* in New York City are portraits and marble busts of the twelve Caesars, as well as mosaics, bronze medallions, and a silver water tankard designed from authentic Roman coins.

Campbell Soup Company's first restaurant venture on the East Coast had a western motif, spaciousness, and good lighting to help achieve a family type atmosphere for its steak specialty restaurant.

Hanover Trail emphasized a western motif through the use of wood beams, tavern lamps, and rustic wall decorations. What's more, each of the dining rooms has a western name: Sioux City and Kansas City. The cocktail lounge is called Dodge City, while the Bull Pen accommodates large parties. The room also has see-through paintings of the West that patrons can view from either side. Among the decorations are steerhide skins, indian blankets, steer horns, wooden indians, a wagon wheel lamp, and old-fashioned milk cans that function as ash trays.

Bonanza, Black Angus, and *Ponderosa*—steak specialty restaurants—all appeal to the family trade through western motifs.

O'Leary's in Chicago has an 18th century motif, with antique chairs and tie-back curtains. The menu features a rotation of ethnic meals—Irish, German, Italian. To attract Monday patronage, it offers a $2.75 menu special.

Nantucket Cove in Chicago has the appearance of a fishing village, complete with authentic wood, rope, and artifacts from Nantucket Island. There are also pictures of whales.

Sage's East of Chicago has an authentic English atmosphere in three spacious rooms. Even its variety of dishes have British names.

PERSONNEL

Your employees constitute a vital image-forming function. Robert Farrell, President of *Farrell's Ice Cream Parlor,* once commented that, "If you put hundreds of thousands of dollars into your restaurant and you don't take the time to train and motivate a two-dollar-an-hour employee, it'll ruin you."

Robert Sikora, President of Bobby McGee's Conglomeration, said he makes every effort to maintain employee enthusiasm at high gear in his eight southwestern restaurants. Waiters and waitresses and other service personnel are dressed in a variety of costumes to lend a "fun" atmosphere for the enjoyment of both the customers and the employees. (Several years ago, Mr. Sikora actually purchased the entire inventory of a Hollywood costume maker.)

Many restaurateurs have achieved an image of having "happy" and concerned personnel by letting their employees become involved in the planning and policy-making of the restaurant. Providing employees with both a sense of responsibility and—equally important—

of accountability, you can encourage them to work hard at pleasing the customer and to take a personal interest in the welfare of the restaurant.

Forum of the Twelve Caesars in New York gives its chef "top billing" in its ads. These ads feature his supervisory control over his domain and promise the customer "wonderful things." This kind of publicity performs the dual role of building employee morale and keynoting your personnel as an important image-making factor of your restaurant.

UNIFORMS

Service attire is now considered an important part of establishing a restaurant's image. Rather than the traditional, off-the-shelf uniforms, many costumes now conform and add to the dining theme. This has the effect of transporting the customer into a fantasy world while he is dining in your restaurant.

California's *Marina del Rey* has successfully provided the kind of creative personnel attire that transforms the restaurant into a theatre. The costumes vary, according to the special theme of each of its eighteen units.

DRAMATIZE YOUR FOOD

Food has universal appeal and lends itself to various forms of dramatic showmanship. For example, consider the way it's prepared, how it's served, its appearance, quality, and packaging.

Some years ago one New York restaurant featured scrambled eggs, prepared on a stove in its window by a chef all in uniform. The preparation had all the visual excitement of a theatrical performance, even exceeding the showmanship of pizza-throwing. The eggs were heaped high on the plate, fashioned into an attractive pyramid design. Everyday scrambled eggs then resembled something different—a work of art, a dining delight. The window performance was constantly watched by a standing-room-only crowd that literally gasped with astonishment and admiration.

While everyday foods may seem hard to show with drama, even

such common items as hamburgers benefit from a dramatic display. Many restaurants prepare them in the window to entice passers-by, who can view their leanness and plumpness and practically smell their aroma. When you take the time and effort to make your foods more appealing, suddenly customers find it "different" from your competitor's. This prompts them to come in and order from you.

Customers particularly love the showmanship of serving food. Flaming shaslik of cherries jubilee; sizzling steaks or Chinese rice: They never fail to arouse customer delight. Neither does a Caesar's salad that is prepared at the table before the patron's eyes with skill and finesse. Benihana's used this showmanship to build up an enormously successful chain.

Provided it is presented well, a salad bar can not only display creativity and uniqueness, but can be—and in many cases is—the major drawing card of very successful operations.

COMMUNITY PROJECTS

Cooperating with businessmen around the community can be profitable all around. For example, get together a group, including the motion picture theater owner, the bowling alley proprietor, and others, and join efforts to offer a "Night on the Town" for an all-inclusive price.

Or you might get together with one of the chain store operators in your town and offer a free meal in your restaurant to whoever holds a certain numbered checking ticket from his store. If both of you give enough publicity to this project, it can generate a considerable amount of interest.

You might even want to suggest that your restaurant provide the setting for a department store spring or fall fashion show. You would probably want to offer this at a luncheon, where you could expect to draw large feminine patronage. Work with the store in preparing announcements and advertisements: Here is where you can go all out in newspapers, radio, and television ads.

It is up to the store to provide the models, the emcee or announcer, and the taped music. You plan satisfactory display space, a runway that can be seen from all over the dining room, and a backstage dressing room, where the models can dress and change quickly and efficiently. If your community is a large one, the store will probably engage professional models. However, in smaller places, local women may volunteer to act as models.

If possible, try to get the local television station to cover this event. And, of course, join with the store in an effort to get all fashion editors of the vicinity invited as guests and seated at tables most suitable for viewing the show.

You can make use of such a show in a number of ways. Is one of the guests an excellent prospect for group business? Then why not concoct a special dish and name it in his company's honor, such as Beef a la Reliance (or Beacon, or whatever the company's name is)? When the dish is ready and tested, invite the guest or the officers of the company to a special dinner or lunch, featuring, of course, the new dish.

Often this will encourage return business. If this company holds a convention, a sales meeting, a luncheon, dinner, or banquet on your premises, give them a private dining room, naming it for the company and occasion "Reliance Room," with appropriate signs and decorations.

QUALITY CONTROL

As any restaurateur will attest, among the crucial factors that either impede or achieve repetitive patronage is the quality of the food, service, and general appearance of the restaurant. Insuring this quality through proper quality control is vital in achieving a consistently favorable quality image, in inducing return patronage, and in encouraging word-of-mouth advertising.

More and more operations are adopting both innovative and stronger quality control measures. One of the foremost innovators in this field is Sky Chefs, a subsidiary of American Airlines. Sky Chefs is one of the most extensive food purveyors in the country, servicing in-flight meals for some 30 airlines and providing a food service for thousands of travelers daily in its many airport restaurants.

A 25-point quality control standards program has been devised under the direction of Sky Chefs' A. C. Ferrari, President. The program requires observations in the following areas of performance.

Administration—Airline
   catering
Safety procedures
Delay performance
Meal components
Sanitation & housekeeping
Completeness of equipment
Automotive maintenance
Automotive appearance
AFEH appearance
Equipment washing
   machines
Refrigerator/Freezers
Conservation of customer
   equipment
Hot food transporters
On-time arrival

Food handling/Conform-
   ance to specifications
Galley temperatures
Administration—Public
   facilities
Waiter/Waitress
Host/Hostess
Cashier
Bartender
Cocktail waiter/waitress
Snack bar
Sanitation
Service kitchen
Facilities maintenance and
   cleaning
Retail shop

Performance is checked out by the management of each food unit. An error factor from 0–10%, depending on the category, is permitted. In the event that the error factor is greater, a Quality Control Action Form is filled out and dispatched to the Regional Vice President, along with an explanation of what measures have been taken to correct the errors.

As explained by Mr. Ferrari in the Sky Chefs' Quality Control Manual:

> Sky Chefs' Quality Control Program is a positive action program which allows unit management to measure performance based on predetermined standards set by operations and staff personnel.
>
> The purpose of the program is to provide local management with a tool to both measure and improve service to our customers.
>
> In order for our Quality Control Program to be an effective tool, the following requirements must be met:
>
> 1. Observations are to be made by members of management, who must familiarize themselves with the instructions as outlined in the sections applicable to the areas being checked.

2. Catering Kitchen management shall conduct observations in Airline Catering categories and Public Facilities management shall conduct observations in Public Facility categories.

3. Observations must be made on a random basis at various times of the day so that all shifts are included.

4. Reporting must be accurate and accomplished on a systematic basis as set forth in the instructions.

5. Corrective action must be taken immediately on those areas found to be below standard.

6. Management on all levels must become totally involved with the program and view it as constructive and positive.

Mr. Ferrari goes on to say:

> It is not the purpose of our quality control program to "police" unit management. It is rather an Awareness Program. As these standards are checked off and graded daily by the management, there is a growing awareness of the problem areas and corrective measures required—e.g., untidy waitress uniforms, an unclean spatula, and so on. Our main office evaluator appears at each unit, at unscheduled intervals, to recheck the "grades."

Mr. Ferrari states that this program serves the dual purpose of instilling both quality control and enhanced morale among personnel, achieving a sense of team effort. On the following pages are some of the forms that Sky Chef uses to insure proper quality control.

Thus quality control, for restaurants and purveyors alike, is one of the most important factors in projecting a caring, quality management and operation. If you project an attractive appearance, an appealing decor, considerate and helpful personnel, interesting and unusual food preparations, and a quality operation, you have a good opportunity for gaining a large and loyal clientele.

SKYCHEFS

Cafeteria—Observation Record

Unit _____
Month of _____

DINNER

DATE/OBSERVER	1	2	3	4	5	6	7	8	9	10	11	12	13	14	15
a Attendant Personality															
b Personal Appearance															
c Additional Sales Attempted															
d Appearance of Food And Steamtable															
e Clean Tables And Filled And Clean Condiments															
f Menu Board															
g Cash Handling															
h Tableware Available And Clean															
i General Neatness And Cleanliness															
Name or Initials of Individual Observed															
Record Entire Observation as Std. (√) or Below Std. (X).															

Comments:
_____
_____
_____
_____

No. Observations Standard   A   ☐

Total No. Observations   B   ☐

% Monthly Performance   C   ☐
A ÷ B = C
Record C on Line B-7 of Form QSS

SKY CHEFS

Food Handling Procedures/Conformance To Specifications

OBSERVATION NO.	1	2	3	4	5	6	7	8	9	10	11	12	13	14	15	16	17	18	19	20	21	22	23	24	25	26	27	28	29	30
1. Receiving Procedures Followed																														
2. Recipes & Specifications Followed																														
3. Food Handling Procedures Followed																														
4. Cooking Equipment Functioning																														
5. Useable Food Not Discarded																														
6. Over Portioning Controlled																														
7. Over Production Minimized																														
8. Proper Cleaning Habits Followed																														
9. Meals Prepared with Care																														
10. Security & Control Adequate																														
OBSERVATION STANDARD (✓) OR BELOW STANDARD (X)																														
OBSERVERS INITIALS																														

Indicate Observation as
Standard (✓) or Below
Standard (X) in the
appropriate columns.

A. No. Observations Standard

B. Total Observations

C. % Monthly Performance
A ÷ B = C

Record this figure
on line A-14,
Form QSS

QC-265 REV. 1-75

SKYCHEFS

AFEH Uniform Appearance Performance

Unit _____

Month of: _____

DATE / OBSERVER	1	2	3	4	5	6	7	8	9	10	11	12	13	14	15	16	17	18	19	20	21	22	23	24	25	26	27	28	29	30
Shirt: Sky Chefs Specs A																														
Pants: Sky Chefs Specs B																														
Bump Cap: Specs With Logo Affixed C																														
Security Badge Visible D																														
Torn or Dirty Clothes Worn E																														
Haircut, Sideburns or Mustache per local Management F																														
Initials of Driver/Helper G																														
Record entire Obs. as Std. (✓) or Below Std. (X)																														

OBS. NO. , ACTION TAKEN & DATE OF REVIEW

No. Observations Standard A. ☐

Total No. Observations B. ☐

% Monthly Performance C. ☐
A ÷ B = C

Record on
Line A-8 of
Form QSS

QC-259 REV 1-75

Automotive Appearance Check Sheet

SKYCHEFS

UNIT _____
MONTH _____

OBSERVATION NO.	1	2	3	4	5	6	7	8	9	10	11	12	13	14	15	16	17	18	19	20	21	22	23	24	25	26	27	28	29	30
DATE/VEHICLE NO.																														
1. EXTERIOR OF VEHICLE CLEAN																														
2. INTERIOR OF VEHICLE CLEAN																														
3. PAINT, DECALS IN GOOD CONDITION																														
4. SEATS: SECURE, MAINTAINED																														
5. NO SMOKING SIGN DISPLAYED IN CAB																														

OBSERVERS INTIALS

Entire Observation
Standard (✓) or Below
Standard (X), (2 or More
(X) = Below Standard)

A. No. Observations Standard

B. Total No. Observations

C. % Monthly Performance
   A ÷ B = C

Record on Line A-7 of Form QSS

OBS. NO.	COMMENTS	OBS. NO.	COMMENTS

QC-258 REV. 1-75

SKY CHEFS

Automotive Maintenance Check Sheet

UNIT _____   VEHICLE NUMBER _____

DATE _____   OBSERVER _____

OBSERVATIONS	W T	BELOW STD. (X)	COMMENTS
1. HAND AND MICRO BRAKE OPERABLE	3		
2. LIFT OPERABLE	3		
3. FOOT BRAKES MINIMUM PLAY	3		
4. TIRE TREAD ACCEPTABLE	2		
5. LIGHTS/DIRECTIONALS OPERABLE	2		
6. HORN OPERABLE	1		
7. WINDSHIELD WIPERS OPERABLE AND IN GOOD CONDITION	1		
8. REAR DOOR, GATE OR CHAINS WORKING PROPERLY	1		
9. CHOCK AVAILABLE AND SECURED	1		
10. REFLECTORS INSTALLED	1		
TOTAL POINTS – STANDARD (✓) OR BELOW STANDARD (X)			Record (✓) or (X) on Auto Maintenance Performance Recap.

3 POINTS OR MORE = BELOW STANDARD OBSERVATION

CORRECTED BY _____

QC-256 REV. 1-75

SKY CHEFS

Vehicle Safety Procedure Check List

UNIT _____ DATE: _____
TIME: _____
FLIGHT #: _____
A/C TYPE: _____
AIRLINE: _____
TYPE VEHICLE: Highlift _____ Van _____
DRIVER/HELPER: _____ / _____

	STANDARD (✓)	BELOW STANDARD (X)	COMMENT
1. Brakes Checked Before Vehicle Use			
2. No Sharp Turns, Take Offs or Stops			
3. A/C Stopped Before Vehicle Approach			
4. Approach Speed Limits Observed			
5. Full Stop at Wing Accomplished			
6. Guideman Used—Correct Hand Signals			
7. Full Stop at 8 Feet Accomplished			
8. Wheels Chocked			
9. Driving Rules Observed			
10. Park Brake Set			
11. Cabin Door Closed While Raising Vehicle			
12. Rear Opening Closed			
13. Deadman Control Not Blocked			
14. Pod Cover Used (727-223 Aircraft)			
15. A/C Door/Service Unit Clearance Observed			
16. Proper Back-off Procdures Observed			
17. Vehicle Not Driven Between A/C & Terminal			
18. Engine Off—Unattended Vehicle			
19. Drivers File Checked			

Standard (✓) [   ]

Below Standard (X) [   ]

Record Standard (✓), Below Standard (X) on Vehicle Safety Procedure Performance Recap ·

QC-251 REV. 1-75

SKYCHEFS

Sky Chefs Quality Statistics Summary

Date _____ 197 ___

AIRLINE CATERING	STD	BNA	BOS	CLE	CVG	DFW	DEN	DTW	ELP	HNL	ITK	JFK	LAX	LFP	LGA	OKC	ORD	PDX	PHX	RFK	ROC	SFO	SYR	TUL	TUS	TWK	TYS
A-1 Safety Procedures	100																										
A-2 Delay Performance	99.8																										
A-3 Meal Components	95																										
A-4 Sanitation/Housekeeping	90																										
A-5 Completeness of Equip	95																										
A-6 Auto Maintenance	90																										
A-7 Auto Appearance	90																										
A-8 AFEH Appearance	93																										
A-9 Equip. Wash. Machines	93																										
A-10 Refrigerators/Freezers	93																										
A-11 Cons of Cust. Equip	93																										
A-12 Hot Food Transporters	93																										
A-13 On Time Arrival	95																										
A-14 Food Handling/Specs	93																										
A-15 Galley Temperatures	95																										

PUBLIC FACILITIES	STD	BNA	BOS	CLE	CVG	None	DEN	None	ELP	None	JFK	None	LFP	None	OKC	None	PDX	PHX	None	ROC	None	SYR	TUL	TWK	TYS
B-1 Waitress/Waiter	90																								
B-2 Hostess	90																								
B-3 Cashier	90																								
B-4 Bartender	90																								
B-5 Cocktail Waitress	90																								
B-6 Snack Bar	90																								
B-7 Sanitation	90																								
B-8 Service Kitchen	90																								
B-9 Maintenance & Cleaning	93																								
B-10 Retail Shops	90																								

QC-248 REV. 3-76

Chapter 4

Off-Premises Sales

You've done everything possible with the money and human energy you have to make your restaurant a desirable place to eat. The decor charms the eye; the food pleases the palette; the service blends promptness with courtesy; the image perfectly suits the market's needs. It is, in your opinion, all that a diner could ask for.

However, you still may not have as many customers as you can serve. Every week, every month, every season may bring unexpected lulls in business when the overhead is there, but the customers aren't.

Relying on off-the-street trade or on an impulsive decision by passing motorists frequently leads to empty tables. If you want a constant, dependable clientele, you have to go out and look for it.

DEVELOPING A SALES PROGRAM

Reaching out for customers rather than depending on impulsive passerby traffic is off-premises salesmanship. Phone calls, office visits, letters, ads, social encounters: These are your tools. To be effective, they must be employed systematically and according to a prearranged plan. Above all, they must be aimed at your particular market. This naturally requires you to know who your market is. It is primarily family trade or business trade? Teenagers? College students? Others? There's a whole wonderful world of people who get hungry three times a day—a world of different appetites and different needs to be satisfied by you.

To develop a knowledgeable off-premises sales program, you should be thoroughly acquainted with your potential market. This may be difficult to determine without considerable study and effort. Find out the age group, affluence, and interests of your potential clientele. Also consider the future. Find out if a particular industry is considering relocation in your area.

A sales program need not be expensive. When you know your market and your budget, you're ready to plan your media strategy. You might have to choose between newspaper, direct mail, radio, television, or telephone advertising. If your budget is large enough to include all of these media, balance each of these outlets so that they reach different parts of your total audience at the optimum time.

Generally speaking, don't sink your budget into a one-shot campaign. You don't want to depend on a narrow range of clientele. Program a regular series of mailings, radio commercials, magazine and newspaper ads. Don't expect immediate results; nor should you rely on a lucky streak to magically continue business without a push from you. More often than not, regular and persistent efforts will bring profitable rewards.

Here are some suggestions for off-premises sales. You'll find many more of your own, depending on your circumstances.

1. Make constant business contacts.
2. Place your brochures on counters of neighboring businesses. You'll be surprised how many will consent; try asking.
3. Write down the dates of all contacts. Update and expand this file.
4. Make use of civic and fraternal organizations.
5. There is no such thing as an "inactive" community. Any community that qualifies sitewise for your restaurant will also have fraternal, political, and civic organizations. These constitute prime potential customers and referral generators.

6. Get to know social and civic leaders. Their organizations hold luncheons or dinners on special occasions. These contacts are particularly important if you have private dining rooms. Remember that political campaigns can continue for several months. During this time a candidate's inner circle meets constantly. They need a place—perhaps a special table —where they can be seen but not overheard while they combine lunch with a strategy-planning session. Meeting this need can mean regular business for you.

7. Contact the Chamber of Commerce. Most visitors to your community will stop there for information, maps, and recommendations for a good meal.

8. Leave brochures there. Also become personally acquainted with the person behind the desk. Having a friend in an important place never hurts and often increases business.

ORGANIZATIONS AND COMMITTEES

Can you handle large groups in your restaurant? Every organization that meets regularly has committees that even occasionally meet over dinner. Campaign workers work long hours—a lucrative market if you have take-out service, or, better yet, if you can deliver meals to headquarters. Off-premises services should be prominently noted on your cards and brochures.

LOCAL GAS STATIONS

"Know a good place to eat around here?" is a common question among people who travel by car: tourists, salesmen, or day visitors. Since about forty percent of all automobile travel occurs after dark, the local filling station is a logical place to get such information. If he sees enough of you, the attendant is sure to think of your restaurant first. And if you leave brochures and cards, you'll give the attendant a chance to provide even more service for his customers. Talk to him about your restaurant. Could be, he'll turn out to be a very valuable friend.

SECONDARY AIRPORTS

One important rule to remember about secondary airports is: Give 'em first class service. If you're not far from a secondary airport, make sure you cater in part to people involved in this business. More private aircraft fly today than planes operated by the scheduled airlines. A big chunk of this market is business aircraft. Small, local, commercial airlines and air taxi services also contribute to the flourishing stream of traffic taking off and landing at the secondary airport.

The airport manager can be one of your most lucrative contacts. Make an appointment with him, and come prepared with a concise description of your restaurant and its facilities. There's a lot to be learned from him. Find out the companies that use the field and how often; the number of employees that come and their position in the firm; peak traffic hours for businesses; where the recreational fliers come from; how the percentage of traffic differs between recreational and business users; and how long plane commuters stay in town. Then put all of the answers into the card file. Develop a profile of your steadiest market, accumulating information from varied contacts that will help you learn about various groups among your clientele.

Inform the manager when you make special arrangements for groups, whether they involve setting up private rooms or offering lower group rates. Leave post cards and brochures for the manager to pass out to interested customers. And be sure to keep an eye open for promotional material that you can pin up on local industrial bulletin boards. Return regularly with a fresh supply of brochures and bulletin board material.

RAILROADS AND OTHER PUBLIC TRANSPORTATION

Trains and buses are heavily used for both long-distance travel and for shorter runs in densely populated urban areas. Since it is likely that public transportation will increase throughout the country in the future, make the very best use of it that you can.

First, leave brochures with the attendant and at the information desk. Second, tack a sign on to a bulletin board. Third, advertise on billboards and in train cars. Fourth, contact the railroad advertising department and ask where free space is available. Since commuters travel regularly by train or bus, they soak up the advertising around them between catnaps, poker games, work, and conversation.

Repeat these steps at bus depots and airline terminals. Look for quiet corners beyond the main waiting room where passengers lounge while they wait for their plane or bus, and where their eyes fall on your advertising or promotional material.

Don't forget to return and check to see that there are still enough brochures and that your signs are still there. Write down the date that you came and the material you left for future reference.

THE TOLL BOOTH: A TRAVELER'S GUIDE

Motorists often ride long stretches of highway before finding a place to stop and ask about the road ahead. A toll booth attendant might be his only source of information at night or in isolated areas. And a good one. Toll booth attendants usually come from the area they work in and know where a tired motorist can stretch his legs under a table laden with appetizing food. Get to know him; drop off a few brochures and cards. Toll booth attendants must keep traffc moving. When travelers ask advice, see that the first restaurant he thinks of is yours.

CAR RENTAL AGENCIES

Car rental agencies provide a host of services besides a smile and a car. They're often the first place out-of-towners rush to after stepping off a plane or train. Make your restaurant one of his first contacts after renting a car by paying a friendly visit to the booth and by leaving brochures.

Talk to the manager, not only to get permission to leave brochures, but also to cultivate an ongoing relationship. He is a vital source of information on the kind of visitors that come to your community. Are his customers primarily business people or families? How often do they come? From where? When are his busiest seasons?

Have a small, well-designed sign available just in case he has a bulletin board. Here's a contact you can exchange favors with. If you have a bulletin board with information that can be helpful to your customers, take back some of the car rental brochures and put them up in your restaurant.

FINANCIAL INSTITUTIONS

Bankers are among the most widely respected and well-known leaders in any community. They are also aggressive business people, the first to know of new incoming business and industry. They often have an accurate picture of economic change in your region. This can help you keep abreast of what's happening, both in your own community and outside.

What's more, out-of-town executives are likely to ask for their banker's recommendations for a good meal. With his wide range of contacts, a banker can be a terrific salesman—for you.

GOVERNMENT AGENCIES MEAN BUSINESS

Knowing the mayor and local government officials personally can offer numerous benefits, since government permeates the economy of even the smallest town. Even minor officials may know of large state or federally funded projects that will affect the entire community, including your restaurant.

During the long planning phase for new government transportation, housing, defense, or environmental facilities, carloads of consultants will be visiting your area. Advance knowledge of their visit gives you an inside track on issues affecting your business and area.

LOCAL HOSPITALS

A hospital is the nucleus of a community. Hospital corridors swarm with patients' relatives, transients involved in accidents, out-of-town specialists, representatives of drug or hospital equipment and supply companies. Develop friendly relationships with strategic personnel at the hospital like receptionists, pharmacists, and administrators—any personnel in frequent touch with hospital visitors. Leave your literature at the information desk, on a bulletin board, or in the gift shop—wherever the hospital makes space available. And don't forget a thank you note or even a small, occasional gift when diners have been referred to you by helpful personnel there.

FUNERAL HOMES

Funerals are not only mournful events, but life-enriching as well, since they are often the motivating reason for an infrequent family re-union. In their bereavement, the immediate family is likely to rely on the funeral director's recommendation on where to dine or where to get take-out food from. So a funeral party can keep your kitchen very busy. Therefore, it might be wise to meet the funeral director and give him a tour of your restaurant.

DON'T LET TRUCKERS PASS YOU BY

Legend has it that truckers know good food. You want business from these truckers, but more likely than not your parking facilities can't take his rig. What's more, you probably don't want his truck gracing the front of your establishment or discouraging automobile traffic. Investigate the user of any large space in the rear of your estab-lishment for truck parking. If that is impossible, try to make financial arrangements with a nearby auto park or with a neighboring business that has the space: Perhaps they'd like to share both the space and the finances.

You may also be near enough to a truck terminal to make soliciting business worthwhile. If so, become acquainted with the man-agers. They can provide a list of trucking firms based at this ter-minal. If they are interested in seeing your restaurant, give them a cook's tour—or a public relations dinner.

Communicate directly with trucking firms using surrounding highways. Get their names and addresses from passing trucks. Send brochures with covering letters stressing the hearty food, big portions, and fine taste of your menu.

Any trucking firm with a steady clientele at your restaurant warrants special consideration. Attracting "trucker" business can help to generate steady, profitable patronage. You may even want to con-sider offering reduced rates, since truckers are budget-minded, and you may be competing with other restaurants in your area. Truckers, by the way, are splendid referral sources. If they like a place, you'll reap valuable word-of-mouth advertising benefits.

UNIONS

If your employees are not unionized, you can bypass this one, but don't miss the opportunity if they are. An active union not only provides many services for its members, but in some areas also serves as an informal place to socialize. Ask if you can leave brochures and a notice on a bulletin board. Unions are very big on brotherhood. Your message should imply support of unionism.

HOUSE HUNTERS

Second homes, summer homes, or new homes with a new life or job: The search takes time. House hunters browsing through your area might remain for a weekend or a week, enough time for them to get hooked on your superlative cuisine.

Get in touch with real estate agents. Sit down for a few minutes with the manager in the buying office of a new development and leave brochures in your wake. Advertise on the particular day when the local newspaper carries the greatest number of real estate ads. The chamber of commerce, too, of course, will have your brochures and your restaurant at the top of their list.

Smooth the way to your restaurant for new arrivals. Include a map on the brochure. Stress family-oriented features such as children's portions or special dinners. Publicize your proximity to shopping and recreational areas. These are the kind of things that people who are thinking of moving your way will want to see.

One last note: A fairly nice bonus comes from satisfied tourists and tour guides whose word-of-mouth advertising costs you nothing.

GET DOWN TO BUSINESS

It is said that more business deals are made over lunch than at the office. This is particularly apt among local industry people. In conversations with your friends around town, ask for news about any companies that are planning large meetings and may need more space than the office provides. When you're talking to executives, casually remind them that you have private dining rooms or certain tables that are set apart for discreet conversations, which can be reserved for any future date.

SALES MEETINGS

A company with a large sales staff is likely to have at least one general meeting a year. There will also be meetings to introduce new products or to deal with regional sales.

Make an appointment to see the head of the firm or the top sales executive. Give a brief account of the advantages your restaurant has; perhaps it is within walking distance of the plant. Your promotional literature should reflect the high quality and service of your restaurant. Ask if a few pieces can be left with the person responsible for making reservations for visiting company personnel. Show concern for the executive's idea of what his needs are. Ask questions.

However, a single interview with no follow-up phone call, letter, or visit is time wasted. Send personalized letters outlining the points you've made about your restaurant: private rooms, unique cuisine, catered meals at corporate offices, free parking, whether reservations are required, acceptable credit cards, and whether your restaurant can be rented for a private party. These are often the most important considerations for busy executives who have little time to find these things out themselves. Enclose a brochure and any other descriptive literature that points out the features of your restaurant that coincide with needs of the firm. Personalize the letter as much as possible by including facts you've picked up about the company during the interview.

Round out your campaign with ads in trade and professional publications that will reach firms who do business in your area. Suggest that on visits to a prominent local firm—and name it—your restaurant should also be on the schedule. You'll be creating business and good will—both at the same time.

However, be sure to check with the local firm first before using its name. Some firms have a policy against being mentioned in advertising they do not control. Make clear to the firm that you will pay all expenses for the ad. Don't push if the reaction is negative. However, if you sense that the question is negotiable, you might be able to change their minds by offering to show them the ad copy for approval. If they like it, they might even offer to split the cost with you.

Maybe you'd like more weekend business in a slack season, and you know of a firm who wants to hold an important meeting on the weekend. Convey the idea of using your restaurant to exchange ideas in a relaxed atmosphere.

A word of caution: Never promise more than you can deliver. If tables are close together, you cannot offer privacy. Although your place may have other very definite charms, this is not one of them. Stress the positive points you have, but don't lie; it only invites disappointment.

COMPANY TRAINING PROGRAMS

Just about every large company runs training programs. The financial and technological complexity of today's world demands instant specialists that can be readied for their corporate roles as quickly as possible. Programs might be as short as two weeks or as long as several months. You'll want to know the firms in your area that have training schools. See the man in charge. Perhaps the company winds up its training programs with a dinner for trainees.

USE FOLDERS TO SOLIDIFY YOUR BUSINESS IMAGE

If you're in the hub of business activity, an extra investment in a color brochure for business clientele might clinch the businesslike aura you've set out to convey. Include photographs of your interior and exterior, illustrating their ambience, uniqueness, and flexibility. For example, show a room first as a dining area, and then as a meeting room, with chairs and tables arranged for organization or sales meetings. Give the dimensions of the room, the seating capacity, the rates, and any extras, such as renting slide projectors or blackboards. Consider the possibility of including a menu and a map in your folder.

If you have a successful history of business dinners and meetings, ask if you can use the names of your previous customers. Very special features might even be worthy of a newspaper story or a trade magazine item.

TRAVELING SALES REPRESENTATIVES: A GOLDMINE OF REPEAT BUSINESS

In their restless lives, sales representatives appreciate a familiar environment where they are known and where they can count on good food and service.

Suppliers for local firms send representatives to your area all the time. Get their names from the local firm. Send them literature and offer to show them your establishment next time they're in town. If the supplier is potentially a very valuable source of business, include a meal in the tour. Advertise in industry publications to reach these out-of-town suppliers: "When you visit the (blank) company, relax over the better-than-home-cooking at (your restaurant)."

Sales people are year-round business. Don't brush them off lightly during your peak summer tourist months. If they're regular customers when you need business, make every effort to accommodate them. If your business is "standing room only" in July, let your sales person know, and encourage advance reservations.

NEW CONSTRUCTION, NEW CUSTOMERS

The construction industry is the leading indicator of the American economy. When construction is down, we're all in trouble; when it rises, you can believe those rumors about economic recovery. One of the reasons for the unique place of the construction industry in our economy is the number of jobs it generates. It requires engineers and architects through surveyors, subcontractors, blue-collar workers, lawyers, and loan officers.

That's a lot of appetites. When a construction project near you is about to start—and planning begins long before the first hole in the ground is evident—mail brochures with covering letters welcoming the architects, developers, site managers, and government officials; in short, everyone connected to the project, to your community, and telling them how pleased you'll be to serve them. To find out the names of these companies, watch the financial section of your local news-paper. If you know more than the newspaper does, double-check your information before writing to a government agency or a bank, for instance. The bigger the construction job, the more people involved, and the more effort you will have to expend to capture their patronage.

WOMEN: A NOTE

Never assume that a woman you're talking to is an unimportant worker or a secretary. She might just be the decision-maker who controls the large expense account tabs you want to adorn your restaurant. Just as you wouldn't base your actions on preconceived notions of what to expect from men, don't do so with women.

Of course women are a major part of the vast, untitled pool of employees. Treat them with respect. Their names should be in your card index along with everyone else you send cards to.

COLLEGE ENROLLMENT: INTERVIEWS AND REGISTRATION

Early in the year college campuses bustle with applicants. They and their parents make the rounds of interviews and campus tours. Some of these high school seniors will be back in the fall for enrollment. From that first visit to the time when they graduate, students can become your loyal patrons on big dates and special occasions.

Visit the college or university registrar's office. Inquire what events take place at an off-campus location, such as banquets for parents and children. If the school prepares kits with information on the town, you might offer whatever material you have on your restaurant.

EXTRA COLLEGE CREDITS

Academic institutions seethe with activity: athletic events, lectures, concerts, conferences, art shows, theater, dances, graduation, and a mixed population of students, professors, office personnel, visiting parents, artists, academics, and consultants. Keep up with the campus schedule. Advertise in the school paper. Drop off brochures at central locations: faculty rooms, bulletin boards, dormitories. Meet the athletic director. If you can find out what departments generally hold large dinners, you might suggest your establishment.

Press conferences are a rare but not improbable event. Perhaps you can offer your establishment at no cost to the university. That way you make a civic contribution to, say, science, gathering some free publicity along the way. A similar approach can be used at junior colleges, private schools, and other educational institutions.

LOCAL EVENTS

Every town has its own traditions and communitywide social and athletic events. Dining out goes along with these festivities. Ask around about these events and splurge on some publicity geared to the occasion.

Testimonial Dinners

Honoring departing employees or members of a group is a time-honored tradition. When you learn of these impending events, get the name of the person or department organizing them. Send a brochure and letter. Meet with the person in charge, suggesting your restaurant as the place to hold the banquet. Have sample menus on hand, including the cost of various meals for different sized groups. If there's room for live music or entertainment, mention this. Throw in something new: Supervised child-care for parents who might otherwise have to stay home might pay off handsomely.

Once you succeed in getting a company's business for the big annual affair thrown by a local organization, you're likely to get their business again; next year at this time, they will probably come to you.

Sports and Tournaments

Physical exertion begets big appetites. Make the rounds of private clubs, bowling alleys, ice-skating rinks, ski areas, and develop friendly relationships with the managers. If you are on good terms, you'll know when the big tournaments are coming up as surely as you know the manager's name.

When a team is involved, such as bowling, send a letter and brochure to the team captains suggesting your restaurant for a victory celebration. However, these arrangements are sometimes better done through the manager of the sports facility. Remember that his good will is vital to you. Send all sports people brochures and mailings, regardless of whether they've made it to the finals. Finally, remember that spectators also eat; reach them through ads in tournament programs.

New Car Introductions

Automobile dealers are an aggressive lot, interested in new ways to capture public attention that can lead to greater sales. Use your parking lot to show the annual change in auto models. Make it a local festivity that can give spillover business to your restaurant.

Drape the cars in brightly colored flags for the unveiling before press and public. Set up decorative refreshment stands. Whet the public appetite with newspaper ads and handbills. Feature menu specials named for new car models. Keep balloons floating and a searchlight on into the evening. In short, make it one of the biggest local events of the season.

You might not want it to seem as if you're endorsing one brand of car over another. If parking facilities allow, you might even want to show new models from all local dealers at the same time.

Fairs

Once considered a rural festivity, fairs have spread to city streets. No matter where they are held, they are a melange of entertainment and salable goods with a local orientation. Create good will by offering a raffle, with dinner for two at your restaurant as the prize.

Publicize your food by setting up a booth. Food is a constant best-seller at fairs. Sponsor a potato race or some other competition where fun is more important than winning, and present the Eastwell Restaurant loving cup to the winner. Bring promotional literature to wherever the fair is coordinated from and where booth managers are likely to visit.

Golf Tournaments

You know all the important people in town; in fact, you yourself are one of the important people in town. Enhance your reputation by starting an annual local golf tournament if there isn't one already. A basic requirement, of course, is a local golf course of high quality. Sponsoring a golf tournament is no job for a loner. Prize money must be raised from several contributors. And you'll need the cooperation of the Chamber of Commerce and of the entire business and social community to pull off an event that will do you and your community proud.

Golf is a major national amateur sport played by presidents, executives mixing recreation and work, and just about everybody. It's the kind of event that can command a large audience not only within the local community, but outside as well. There will be more than enough business to go around. Other restaurant owners, motel owners, and sporting goods dealers should be good sources for coworkers on the project. It's the kind of thing sports editors of local papers and radio and television stations love to follow. But to get all these happy results, make sure the project is feasible from the start.

PROMOTIONAL ODDS AND ENDS

Offer a Children's Special

Show your sensitivity to family trade by cutting the check without sacrificing quality. Smaller portions for children at half the price can make a big difference for families with more than one child. This kind of special attention to your customers makes you their first choice when deciding on where to eat out.

Gift Certificates

Gift certificates are the highest form of praise and promotion. The giver is expressing in very definite terms his high regard for your establishment. Gift certificates are usually associated with Christmas, but are often given for birthdays and other personal occasions. The certificates can be made out for family dinners or dinners for two.

Use certificates for your own gift list. Send them to people who regularly refer guests to you. If the certificates are R.S.V.P., you'll

Suggesting a gift certificate to company officials:

Dear Sir:

Thinking up interesting gifts for people with whom you do business can be time-consuming. Here's a suggestion that can make things easier.

Present a wonderful dinner in our restaurant. This is one gift that won't be put aside and forgotten. It's original, thoughtful, and personalized!

Look at the special gift menu we've enclosed. It features a wide selection of our most popular dishes. The menu goes with a handsome gift certificate to the person you specify. We'll be glad to do the actual mailing in your name.

The amount on the certificate can be very flexible. It can involve a dinner for two or for an entire family. You can even include cocktails or wine with dinner if you wish. It can be prepaid, or billed to you at a later date.

If you'll call or send a note, we'll be happy to sit down with you or anyone you designate to discuss details.

Very truly yours,

know when your guests are coming so you can be on hand to welcome them personally. Present a bottle of good wine for the occasion or offer brandy after the meal. Your warm hospitality should renew their dedication to your restaurant and their help in attracting new customers. Gift certificates are a miniscule investment in a continued association with valuable business friends.

Write a Newspaper Column

A second career as a newspaper reporter can help your primary occupation as a restaurateur. Your community newspaper might need a brief local gossip column with who's who and who's where. A daily column would probably be too frequent, but perhaps you can manage it once, twice, or three times a week.

Publicizing your restaurant, naturally, is not the point of the column; nevertheless, every so often you can subtly weave in its name. And don't worry about information; once you're started, you'll find plenty of material flowing your way. What's more, in getting information to fill your columns, you'll establish contacts that will fill your restaurant.

Menus on Automobile Windshields

Publicize a new special dinner by printing up attractive flyers. Get a few students from the high school to slip the flyers under windshields wipers of cars parked in shopping centers and on streets.

Chapter 5

Advertising

Advertising means many things to many people. Restaurant advertising, however, consists primarily of attracting diners through the use of available local media. The most important criteria by which you should determine the type of advertising you use are its cost, its audience, your market, and your ability to pay for the ad.

These factors are all interrelated. For example, even if you reach a significant number of people through your campaign, you will be wasting your money if most of them are uninterested in the type of services you offer. Hence, you must know before deciding upon any specific advertising campaign exactly what type of market will want your business and need your services. What is more, you must also weigh the number of prospects you can reach against the costs of reaching them.

MEDIA SELECTION

Most daily newspapers have restaurant columns in which, for a minimum cost (daily or several times a week), you can list your establishment and featured specialties, price range, entertainment, reservations required, address, etc. You will probably also want to feature planned special events and new features such as Thanksgiving dinner, Christmas dinner, a new dining specialty, or the opening of a new garden or room.

When there are several morning and evening newspapers in a city or town, the type of the circulation of each should be investigated before the medium is chosen. Each newspaper, like each business, has its own type of buyers, and campaigns should be laid out to fit the character of the circulation. Campaigns which are successful in one newspaper are not necessarily so in another.

Often entertainment and/or gourmet magazines are published, especially in large communities. These can also bring customers if you cater to the kind of audience that reads such publications. While per line rates in such publications are usually higher than those in daily newspapers, their readership life is longer and the market they reach is more specific.

A restaurateur uses the newspaper and its circulation to help sell his place and its food. He must watch over this medium just as he does his own operation. Within his restaurant he keeps a close watch over his personnel to see that they work efficiently enough to help them pay their salaries and to make a reasonable profit for his operation. If they fail to meet these requirements, he must fire them and hire new workers. In the same way, advertisements must be watched over for their effectiveness: They must either pay profits or get off the payroll.

STRATEGIC PLANNING

Plan your advertising carefully in advance. Accomplish this in the following way:

- Estimate the results desired from your advertising.
- Establish an advertising budget.
- Devise a creative strategy. (What type of ad style and format should you use?)
- Decide which media are specifically geared to your desired customers, and choose the most effective of them.

TACTICAL DECISIONS

In the selection of media consider the wide range of choices available to you that are within your budget and that can produce the best results.

As your primary objective, define your target audience. Ask yourself, "Who do I want as customers?" Decide on what type of advertising copy is most appropriate to the particular image that you seek.

All advertising copy should observe basic rules of eye appeal, simplicity, brevity, straightforwardness, and credibility.

HOW MUCH SHOULD YOU SPEND?

There is no simple formula which will give you the exact number of dollars and cents you should allot to advertising and sales promotion. Much depends on your special situation and, of course, how aggressively you want to pursue more business. However, there are rules of thumb which can give you a general idea of what you should be spending in this area.

The average restaurant allocates about 5% of its total income to advertising and sales promotion. Applying this figure to an "average restaurant," a typical advertising and sales promotion budget might figure something like this:

Projected sales	$200,000
5% allocated to promotion and advertising activities	$ 10,000

The first year of operation, this budget will, of course, have to be figured on the basis of projected sales. However, each succeeding year's budget should be based on the income of the previous year.

USING NEWSPAPERS

Random advertising in newspapers is a waste of time and money. In order to select the right paper, the right day, and the right section of the paper to advertise in, you must know your market thoroughly. Is it

MAJOR CHAIN AD BUDGETS
(dollars in millions)

	PROJECTED 1975		1974		1975	
	Ad $	Ad $ As % Of Total Sales	Dollars Spent	Percent Sales	Dollars Spent	Percent Sales
McDonald's	65.0	3.5	54.0	3.0	46.5	3.0
Kentucky Fried Chicken	60.0	4.5	52.0	4.0	45.8	4.0
Burger King	24.0	4.5	22.0	4.5	19.0	4.5
Hardee's	15.8	5.0	14.9	5.0	14.0	5.0
A & W	15.0	4.0	14.0	4.0	13.0	4.0
Pizza Hut	10.0	4.5	8.5	4.5	7.0	4.5

McDonald's and Kentucky Fried Chicken are projecting slight increases in their advertising budgets as a percentage of sales. Burger King, Hardee's, A & W and Pizza Hut are holding the line. But all six chains are anticipating an upsurge of television advertising.

transient or terminal? Businessmen mostly? Vacationers? Families? These are all-important facts to know.

Examine your investment in terms of the newspaper's ability to reach your best prospects. Then decide which section of the paper can best further your efforts. Most newspapers can provide you with detailed information about their readership to enable you to make these decisions.

Newspapers can be a very effective means of reaching prospects. Whether they are or not in your particular situation depends on your ability to weigh all the pros and cons.

NEWSPAPER ADVERTISING

What makes a good newspaper ad? There are no simple rules. A lot depends on what you want to stress. A lot depends on how much space you can afford to buy. Generally, a consistent program of small space ads is better than a single, one-shot effort. If you plan only a limited program of newspaper advertising, your newspaper space representative can be most useful in helping you plan the ads. If you intend to plunge into a large-scale newspaper advertising program, it may be best to use a competent advertising agency.

Types of Ads

Newspaper advertisements are of two general types: 1) action, and 2) good will. An action ad aims at direct sales. Its success depends on the attention, interest, and desire which it can arouse. If any of these elements are lacking, the customer will not be moved to act, and the space will be wasted.

A good will ad seeks to familiarize prospective customers with the name of the restaurant, as well as its food style and methods of business. It aims at attention and interest and becomes increasingly important to restaurateurs with each passing year as the competition increases.

HOW TO CREATE A GOOD NEWSPAPER CAMPAIGN

The life of a newspaper is only a day, but it appears every day. The copy should, therefore, be short, with the advertisements continuing over several months to be effective. Since readers usually devote only a few minutes to newspapers, advertisements must convey their message in a flash through their headlines and illustrations. The copy should be simple and easily absorbed.

A campaign with advertisements to build up good will should generally run for three to six months and should be followed by the action campaign. This is so that the good will advertisement will prepare the customers, both old and new, for the ideas which will be used in the action campaign.

In any effective ad, the copy, illustration, and layout should be unified around a single idea. This idea must have a fundamental emotional appeal.

Newspaper campaigns, because of daily circulation, can take advantage of local events, activities, or developments which can be linked with the copy, bringing added interest. A local interest series of advertisements, all having the same layout and makeup, are often very effective. New public buildings, society features, entertainment events (professional or amateur), political and sporting events, lectures, educational events, holidays, and seasonal events, well-known personalities, real estate developments, and civic improvements such as new streets, bridges, and parks can all be the focus of interesting and eye-catching ads. The restaurateur with advertising sense will find plenty of material in his own community to provide a focus for such ads, especially since a new slant on familiar events always adds interest and enthusiasm.

Advertisements may be based on any number of appeals: pride in the home, convenience, fear, comfort, sympathy, humor, play, romance, family love, cleanliness, economy, social prestige, beauty, personal appearance and efficiency. All are prime sources to tap.

Emotional appeal is the heart of a good campaign. Good selling copy depends on both the selection of the appeals and your restaurant's association with them. All successful campaigns are carefully balanced between focusing on the product and appealing to the emotion. The degree of attention an ad gets depends on the ingenuity and originality of the idea and wording of the headline.

Status

The Four Seasons, one of New York's most luxurious restaurants, stressed expensiveness and status in its newspaper ad that was

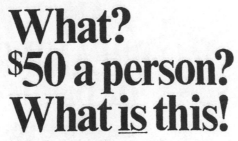

**What?
$50 a person?
What is this!**

It's Le Festival du Champagne!
At The Four Seasons June 7th through June 26th!

It's an unforgettable 6 course dinner. (But the Dinner,
memorable as it will be, is only an excuse for us to
serve you a stunning series of Moët & Chandon champagnes.
Including a Dom Perignon 1969.)

It is an unmatched evening. It is something you should
plan to share with someone you love. We can accept only
30 reservations each evening. (And what a pleased
and satisfied 30 people that will be!)

The two-of-us await you.   Service begins at 7:00 pm.

Tom Margittai

Paul Kovi

THE FOUR SEASONS
99 East 52nd Street PL 4-9494

captioned, "What? $50 a person? What *is* this!" High price—a very
apparent disadvantage and customer-deterrent—was thus converted
into an advantage and a potential customer benefit.

Children

A picture of an adorable, happy, active child unfailingly attracts attention and evokes a positive reader response as well. What's
more, a child's picture in an ad is also a good foil for catchy ad
copy that doesn't sound like every other restaurant's.

A smorgasbord restaurant in New York City captioned the
photo of a lively, grinning child, with, "AM I DREAMING, Or
Did He Say We're Actually Going To The STOCKHOLM?" The

AM I DREAMING Or Did He Say We're Actually Going To

The STOCKHOLM

...It's such a special place I'm sure He will ask me to go steady! ... Will it happen at the romantic ITALIAN TABLE ... or while we are walking around the fascinating SCANDINAVIAN SMORGASBORD TABLE ... Oh life can be so beautiful when you are dining at

The STOCKHOLM

151 W. 51 St. NYC • CI 6-6560

Luncheon • Dinner • Excellent Party Facilities

OFF PREMISES CATERING From 75 Persons & up

Philip Rosen, Managing Director

name of the restaurant was stretched in boldface across the center of the ad beneath the photo, and again near the bottom.

Another New York City restaurant, *The Viking,* captioned its picture "MY HAT'S OFF To A Winner!" above the photo of a child lifting a woman's hat over his head. The first three words, immediately above the photo, worked beautifully with the picture. All-you-can-eat shrimp and chicken dinners were advertised to the side.

While an eye-catching photo is essential, it shouldn't dominate the ad unless three-year-olds are your major clientele. On the other hand, a child's picture can be extremely useful, but only if you ac-

commodate children, since even if you don't mention so in the ad, parents will assume that children are welcome. After all, you are ultimately aiming that ad at parents. After you have caught them with your photo, your caption should lead right into your specialties and unique offerings.

NEWSPAPER IDEAS

Once you decide to embark on a newspaper campaign of your own, there are many ideas you can develop to make your ads more appealing. Take advantage of the special items that you have to offer. Or the special attractions in your community. Got a great chef in the kitchen? Say so. Near a popular beach resort? Say so in the right out-of-town newspapers. Be creative. Don't be content to list your name and address with nothing more. Make people *want* to come.

SUCCESS

You've started six franchises at the request of franchisees. You've catered the diamond jubilee of an important museum or hospital fund-raiser. Film stars carry your salad dressing whenever they go on tour. Six writers have begun books by making notes on your table-cloths. If this is the case, you're probably in the fortunate position of not needing an advertising agency to find something new or good to say about you. (But you might need that agency to say it well.)

A New York City delicatessen restaurant with an overflow waiting line began an ad with, "Thank you for making this ad necessary." It went on to explain that a trailer had been set up for waiting customers where entertainment and free hors d'oeuvres were available.

The restaurant probably would have attracted customers even without the trailer and entertainment. But free hors d'oeuvres are a great inducement to everyone. And along with the trailer and the entertainment, they dramatize an unexpected event.

Like everything else well done, saying you're great takes imagination—imagination that must appeal always to the customer's imagination.

DIRECT MAIL

Direct mail has the advantage of being *direct*. Your sales message goes to the target you have pinpointed. No other advertising medium is more direct. For example, not every newspaper reader is a potential prospect for your services. Nor every radio listener. Nor every motorist who passes by a billboard. But with direct mail you enjoy the advantage of selectivity. You select the people who logically represent sales potential for you. This is not an unqualified endorsement of direct mail over other forms of advertising. You must remember that each medium has its own merits.

There is another unique advantage of direct mail. It can be *personalized*. With your signature, yes. But also catering to the special needs and interests of your prospects. Since you know who you are reaching in advance of the campaign, you can tailor your sales message to a very specific audience. For instance, if you are sending a mailing to local businesses, you can mention not only the company name of the addressee, but also your relationship to and interest in it.

Direct mail tends to suggest mass mailings. However, this is not necessarily the case. One letter can be direct mail. Usually, however, there are many individual prospects who can be reached by mail. These prospects are those who can *send* you business, i.e., local bankers, real estate agents, college officials, and hospital administrators.

Use direct mail. Make it a regular part of your sales development program. It's selective. It's personal. It's inexpensive. And it's profit-making!

A mailing addressed to the "Occupant" is used by many restaurateurs to reach certain selected areas and streets, based on sought-after criteria: wealth, demographics, etc. While this is more economical than getting lists with names, it lacks the personalized touch of individualized name addressing and may therefore be less effective.

Your mailed message should be written in a friendly, interested tone. It should refer to the quality and economy of your food and to any auxiliary features such as entertainment or dancing. You may also wish to include other promotional materials such as introductory discount coupons, sample menus, or brochures.

Dear Sir:

Just a note to express my appreciation to you for choosing to dine at our restaurant.

I sincerely hope that your meal and the service you received were satisfactory. If not, we would certainly appreciate knowing about it.

As you know, the restaurant business is founded on service to customers. So it is important to us to know that we have lived up to your expectations. Otherwise, we might not see you again.

We hope to see you return, and will look forward to your next visit.

Sincerely yours,

Letter to the parents of a birthday child:

Dear Mr. and Mrs. _____ :

    A little bird just told me
that (Name of Child) is about
to celebrate another birthday.
And I should be very pleased
to help make it a happy one if
you would have luncheon or
dinner at our restaurant this
coming Sunday. I have in mind
a special birthday cake made
right here by one of the best
birthday cake bakers in these
parts.

    If you plan to come, please
let me know. We want to be prepared, of course. I believe
there should be (number) candles.
Is my birdie right?

               Sincerely yours,

Letter to a local real estate agent:

Dear Sir:

Among the many details you have to attend to, one of the most frequently asked is, "Know a good place to eat tonight?"

Since your recommendation carries substantial weight, you will naturally wish to direct the party to a restaurant where everything is satisfactory.

Permit me to suggest that you send him or her to our restaurant. If you have ever dined with us, you know that the service is in every respect up to the highest standards. I would very much like to welcome you personally at any time you find it convenient.

I am taking the liberty of enclosing a descriptive brochure. If you need any further information, please call. Meanwhile, I will look forward to accommodating your clients when they come to town.

Very truly yours,

Want a Tested and "Guaranteed"
FORMULA FOR DRAMATIZING YOUR DAY?

Try our coq au vin.
You'll call it the most tantalizing, exciting taste treat you've
ever had. And don't just take our
word for it. Ask our customers.
Or, try our Osso Buco ... or
Shrimp de Gouge ... or steak medallions.
In fact, our entire menu constitutes a pretested formula for
dramatizing your day, giving it
the right momentum, and making it
TRULY DIFFERENT.
You'll also like the comfortable, cozy surroundings, and the
quick, personalized service.
May we prove it to you? Bring
this letter, and enjoy a complimentary cocktail of your choice,
on us.

Cordially,

P.S. We're as close as your phone.
Call for reservations anytime.

DEVELOPING LISTS OF PROSPECTS
FOR DIRECT MAILINGS

In spite of the fact that mailing costs are soaring, direct mailings can often prove the most economical means for reaching the greatest number of your best prospects. Mailing lists of potential customers can be either purchased from other organizations or compiled by knowledgeable individuals. Reliable listing sources will often give them to you in the form of labels that can be pressed onto the envelope containing your promotional material. These can be purchased on the basis of the specific geographical area, occupation, income, or some other aspect of your audience.

Remember, however, that lists become outdated. Addresses in a given community change at an average of about 20% a year. You will find that a street-by-street, avenue-by-avenue telephone directory will keep you pretty much up-to-date in your mailings.

Here are just a few ways to develop mailing lists:

1. *Organization Contracts.* Contact clubs, organizations, and societies in your area. Solicit the patronage of such organizations and their individual members for meetings or banquets, for example.

2. *Newspapers.* Many newspapers have listings of out-of-town subscribers which are available to you for a nominal fee. The out-of-town subscriber is more than likely to have sufficient family, social, or business interests in the community to be an occasional visitor.

3. *Sports Events.* Suppose the local golf club is planning a major tournament. Contact the club. See if you can obtain a list of players and other visitors expected to attend.

4. *Institutions.* At least twice a year colleges and universities attract a large number of out-of-town visitors for graduation ceremonies. Talk with school officials and see if you can obtain a list of the parents of the graduating seniors. They can often be reached in other ways that may prove money-saving to you, such as including your brochure along with the graduation information. Or, if the school sends out a list of general information to them, they may include the

time and place of graduation, the number of guests each graduate is permitted, and even, thanks to your efforts, recommended accommodations.

See? There are many possible sources of direct mail lists. Dwell on it for a while and you'll come up with more ideas than you'll ever be able to use. The trick is to select the ones that represent the surest business potential.

DIRECTORY ADVERTISING

Another type of advertising media which can prove highly effective for a restaurant are the local Yellow Pages and various local business directories. In most areas, the Yellow Pages lists restaurants under ethnic group as well as in an alphabetical listing. You can purchase space relatively inexpensively—anywhere from a few lines to a large fractional at a reasonable cost.

HIGHWAY SIGNS

Highway signs are effective for several reasons.

- They're distinctive.
- They're attractive.
- They're quickly visible from long distances.
- They convey action.
- They quickly identify your restaurant, enabling the traveler to make a quick decision.

The following are some salient facts about outdoor signs and maintaining a sign program that should help you formulate your own program.

- Bear in mind that competition along the highway is fierce. Thousands of signs vie with each other for the attention of the traveling public. And since 85% of all travel is by automobile, it is important that your sign be professionally planned to achieve uniqueness.

• Highway signs should be interesting, but not wordy. Seven to ten words are about all the motorist has time to read comfortably as he passes. So get your message across quickly. If you have several signs up, each one might suggest just one benefit. Remember the Burma Shave signs?

• Signs should be carefully placed to draw attention away from your competition. Choose long stretches of straight road so the motorist has the maximum amount of time to notice and read about you. This is especially necessary for feeder signs—those remote from your location which lead the prospect to you.

• The larger signs are especially necessary near your location to identify your restaurant and give final directions. They are also used to sell meeting and dining facilities, entertainment, etc. This kind of sign is exceedingly important in resort areas where the traffic is terminal rather than transient.

• Since over 40% of all traveling is done after dark, and more than 65% of prospects arrive after dark, it is imperative that an outdoor sign be well lit. At the very least, your signs should contain luminescent materials that reflect passing headlights. They should also be carefully and continually checked and maintained. If the grounds around them become overgrown or the signs themselves are allowed to deteriorate, they lose their effectiveness. Travelers would be justified in concluding that a seedy sign means a seedy restaurant.

SALES PROMOTION ITEMS

There are many useful items which can be distributed to restaurant patrons—either by mail or during a visit to your establishment—which can serve as constant and appreciated reminders of your dining facilities. Calendars can be purchased in quantity at reasonable prices, imprinted with your restaurant's name, address, telephone number, and a line or two of descriptive information. Attractive plastic or wooden swizzle sticks for take-home use that include your restaurant's name, address, telephone number, and a slogan can also be purchased very reasonably in quantity, as can recipe booklets, ballpoint pens, and a host of other items. Here are some examples of imprinted give-aways:

- pens
- pencils
- cigaret lighters
- ashtrays
- flashlights
- memo or address books
- photo albums
- maps
- calendars
- piggy banks
- toilet articles
- swizzle sticks
- mileage booklets
- windshield scrapers
- auto visor attachments
- balloons
- bubble gum
- candy
- thermometers
- calorie counters
- matches
- coasters
- key chains
- desk accessories
- glassware
- salt and pepper shakers
- pot holders
- hot plates
- brushes
- crayons and coloring books
- scissors
- paper dolls
- rubber balls
- stuffed toys
- beach toys
- fans

RADIO AND TELEVISION ADVERTISING

Use of radio and television has become increasingly popular with restaurants, particularly in smaller communities where the rates are more affordable.

Advantages of Radio Advertising

There are many advantages of radio advertising. Among them are the following.

1. It's personalized and can therefore convey a more effective selling message.
2. Showmanship is created by its music and sound effects.
3. It reaches almost every income level.
4. You can pinpoint a particular audience based on the time, station, and program you select to advertise with.

5. Psychologically, hearing often has stronger impact than seeing or reading.

6. There's more "power of suggestion" conveyed through hearing than through reading.

7. There's an intimacy engendered by radio, as if you're chatting on a personal level with the listener.

8. No other commercials compete with yours while you are on the air.

9. The cost of advertising per listener is considerably less than for other media.

Selecting Your Market

Who are the customers you desire to reach for your restaurant? Prepare your program and select the station that will reach this specific market. For example, are they:

Men? Women? Children (up to 12)? Adolescents and young adults? Listeners of middle age or older? Persons in middle- and lower-income brackets? Persons in upper-income brackets? Typical urban listeners? Typical rural listeners?

If you decide to go ahead with radio, it isn't difficult to write good radio commercials of your own. Remember that you're talking *to* people—not *at* them. Make them want to come to your place. Give them reasons why. Remember also that your name, address, and telephone number are important ingredients in any radio commercial. Make this loud and clear, and try to repeat it. Remember that there's no page the listener can look at to double-check this information.

Organize your sales story so that you can attract the attention of the specific markets you desire to reach, arouse interest, and create a desire to hear more. And always, at the end of your ad, suggest "action"; i.e., exactly what you want your audience to do, where, when, and how. When you are writing the ad, keep in mind that you are aiming for the ear, not the eye. Be conscious of building up to a peak and calling for action.

Look at the typical radio commercial on the next page. Study it carefully if you want to try your own hand at writing. It's a good idea to remember that the average 60-second commercial should contain no more than 150 words. Thirty- and twenty-second commercials should contain proportionately fewer words.

But don't forget that you do have help available if you want it. Your local radio station is often glad to assist you in the preparation of any single commercial or campaign of commercials.

Here are some basic rules of thumb for effective radio advertising.

1. Select the station that gives you the greatest power over the area in which your best prospects are located.

2. Time your spot announcements for rush hours: early morning, or late afternoon and evening. This is when you get the highest concentration of adult listeners.

3. Don't try to lump too many different ideas in each commercial. It's a natural tendency to want to get as much as possible for your money. But in radio you can't be effective by attempting to say too much with the limited time available. Instead, try to get across one important thought in each commercial. And, of course, remember to mention your name and location in every commercial.

4. Space your commercials close together. They tend to reinforce each other and lend importance and urgency to your message.

Example of 30 Second Commercial

ANNOUNCER: Wanna try a brand new idea this Sunday? Bring the family to the _____ restaurant for dinner. You'll all enjoy the change, and Mom won't have to cook or wash the dishes afterwards. This Sunday they're featuring a complete five-course steak dinner for only five ninety-eight. Special children's portions; superb cooking. Come on out to _____ restaurant at ____(address)____ . It's a great place to eat.

Advantages of Television Advertising

Television may provide added advantages over radio advertising for the restaurant, since it gives play to two senses: sight as well as sound.

There are four basic types of TV commercials:

1. *Live, integrated.* This is a commercial in which the entire message is presented live by an actor announcer and is specially tailored to blend with the format and character of the TV program.

2. *Live, not integrated.* This type of program is usually presented by an announcer, live, but has little or no relation to the format or character of the show.

3. *Film, integrated.* This is generally filmed and integrated with the format or character of the show.

4. *Film, not integrated.* This is the most frequently used type of TV ad. It can be used for practically any program and any station, conforming to almost any market you seek to reach. This is because it is a filmed commercial, but makes no attempt to integrate with the show.

Criteria for TV Advertising

1. Make your commercial informative. Provide valid reasons (taste, sight, surroundings, service, etc.) for patronizing your restaurant.

2. Have your commercial conform to the mood of the specific program it appears with. If, for example, the program is slow and soft-paced, pattern your commercial to this mood. If it's a loud, fast-paced type of program, strive for a more accelerated pace.

3. In all your ads, strive to demonstrate and describe at the same time. This reinforcement builds conviction and remembrance.

4. Audio and video should enhance each other for greatest impact.

5. Summarize as often as possible. This increases remembrance.

6. Convey a strong sales theme early in the ad.

7. Avoid a presenter who distracts. Too often, the more visible and "powerful" the presenter is, the weaker the commer-

cial impact. The viewer may end up recollecting the presenter, but not the product.

8. Keep the setting authentic and in tune with actual conditions.

9. Color television gives a better opportunity for restaurants to advertise their appearance, products, and services. These selling items can all be enhanced through the effective use of color.

Presutti's *Villa Ristorante,* in Columbus, Ohio, an independent Italian eatery, has launched a series of 10-second TV commercials. The objective of these commercials is to increase public awareness and appeal of the restaurant. The TV commercials are all in cartoon form to make them different from other commercials, thus providing a high probability of recall. Cartoons also become less dated than other commercials, and can therefore be repeated longer, thus achieving production economies.

The first commercial is set in Presutti's kitchen with a cartoon character chef explaining, "How do we cook our superb Italian specialties? With time, patience, and passion!" The second focuses on the menu and its selection: Not all food offered is Italian. Still another commercial stresses banquet facilities, atmosphere, and carry-out service. These are the kind of ideas you should keep in mind when considering commercials for your operation.

Whatever form of advertising you choose, however, give long and careful thought to your message, your market, and the most effective media with which to communicate.

Chapter 6

Publicity and Public Relations

PUBLICITY

Oscar Wilde once remarked, "There's only one thing worse than being talked about, and that's not being talked about." Since you are operating a first class (in its particular category) restaurant in which you've made every effort and spared no expense to provide the tops in food and service to your patrons, you want to be talked about!

What sets publicity apart from advertising is that it's free. Generally, publicity refers to information offered in the media—newspapers, television, and radio—that brings public attention or notice to a particular cause. And what's more, publicity that appears as part of a publication's editorial is taken more seriously by readers than paid advertising.

Publicity requires a good deal of imagination. It means hitting your market where and when it counts. It means getting exposure and visibility—and at no cost!

Get to know who's who among the radio, television, and newspaper people in your area. Alert them when you have something important going on—opening a new branch, instituting a new entertainment policy, or providing facilities for a newsworthy function. Send the press an advance news release or "tip" sheet and invite them to attend. If possible, send the release as part of a press kit, which includes photographs and any additional information which will help reporters to write an interesting article. The news release should be marked with the date of release, and the story should contain the "who," "what," "when," "where," and "why" of the event, as well as your own name and telephone number as contact for further information, if needed.

To some extent, the impact of your publicity effort will be determined by its timing. Your material should arrive at the editor's desk sufficiently in advance of the event, but not so early that your event will be forgotten long before it actually occurs, hidden in the deluge of other material that arrives on the editor's desk each day. Often it's best to send the "tip" sheet three or four days prior to delivering the actual news release and press kit. That way, the editor is prepared in advance to receive your release. And when it does arrive, the release reminds him of the event and reinforces his intention of covering your story.

There are many ways to help assure publicity for your restaurant, particularly if you have a creative urge and some talent for writing. Several restaurateurs write recipe columns for local newspapers. In addition to building their own reputation as chefs and columnists, this permits them to refer to events, features, and other information concerning their own establishments. Others write gossip columns, mentioning guests of note, unusual entertainment, interesting or amusing episodes that occurred in their establishments. Still others have been featured on radio and television programs that discuss food preparation, diet food, or new equipment.

Many community newspapers will welcome a short column of local happenings. If you've got the time to stick with it on a regular basis, you could have a lot of fun and, at the same time, work the name of your restaurant into the column every so often. Once you get started, you'll find yourself receiving plenty of material to use in your column. What's more, the contacts you establish in the course of this work will do even more to help keep your restaurant busy.

Recognizing the value of editorial-like ads, many restaurants run regular news-laden columns in their local papers which they pay for at the usual ad rates. These appear and read like typical newspaper columns. They have proved enormously effective in attracting attention and gaining interest. (See the reprint illustrated on p. 94.)

Remember that the community contacts you establish through your own efforts and through those of your staff can be one of your least expensive and most profitable sources of business.

To help you take advantage of every public relations source available, sample press releases and a sample tip sheet are provided on the following pages. These should help you to write your own when the opportunity arises.

REAL-LIFE EXAMPLES OF SUCCESSFUL PUBLICITY CAMPAIGNS

Don Roth's Blackhawk restaurant was publicized in the *Chicago Tribune* as having a "skyscraper tossed salad." The publicity was reprinted on a 4 × 6 card and passed out to its patrons and prospects. The advertising copy went on to state: ". . . and now, the salad bar is available at lunch, too!" This was enormously successful in drawing a crowd—especially during lunch hours.

Here are some other publicity campaigns that various restaurants promoted:

The *Small Chalet* in Chicago instituted an extensive campaign commemorating its 200-year-old history. Invitations were sent to "fellow Americans" announcing its expression of national pride, which picked up extensive publicity in the newspapers.

Gage and Tollner in Brooklyn found that free publicity outdrew paid advertising for this 96-year-old gaslight era seafood and steakhouse. Once the publicity appeared, according to one patron, "Saturday night looked like New Year's Eve."

Twenty-four hours after *Four Season's* in New York got publicity in local papers for its planned two week long festival, dinner at the 225-seat restaurant was sold out for the whole two weeks.

Unless your story has wide public interest, you should stress newsworthy facts or people, rather than the specifics which apply to your establishment alone. For instance, the newspapers and their readers will be more interested in a publicity release that mentions, "Chamber of Commerce dinner inaugurates new Horizon banquet hall," with the details of which guests were present and who the

An advertisement that looks like an editorial.

BLOWING MY OWN HORN by ARTHUR RIBACK

His Eminence Terence Cardinal Cooke graces the confines of Luchow's, the historic landmark on 14th Street, next Wednesday. The beloved leader of the New York Archdiocese will preside over the annual lighting of the huge Luchow's Christmas tree that has been such a part of New York's holiday scene for 94 years. I have been invited to sit with the Cardinal at this joyous occasion. I'll tell you more about it next week.

Incidentally, if you're like most of us "last minute" people and have not made plans for Thanksgiving dinner, I urge you to make it at Luchow's. Thanksgiving at Luchow's is one holiday you'll not forget. There's festive music from the lusty Oompah Band and gentle Victor Herbert strings; there's award winning gourmet cuisine — but most of all, you'll love the ambience, the setting that has attracted luminaries from every walk of life for these many years — "Show Biz" greats from Lillian Russell to Bob Hope; Industrialists from Diamond Jim to Ari Onassis; Presidents from McKinley through Ford; Labor leaders from Gompers to Gotbaum; Composers from Victor Herbert to Dylan.

O. O. McIntyre, the famed journalist, once commented, "In a changing world, nothing changes at Luchow's." How true!

The Empire State Bldg. provides the cover for New York's largest cabaret-niteclub otherwise known as the Riverboat. Some years ago, the Riverboat management came up with an incredible nite-club plan never duplicated and still hard ot comprehend today. Riverboat said, "Give us one flat amount and we'll provide you with a complete night out of Dancing, Dining (on Steak, no less), Show and (here's the incredible component) All the booze you can properly quaff." Riverboat has presented to N. Y. niteclub audiences such star properties as Count Basie, Ella, Marilyn Chambers, The Monkees.

Riverboat customers constantly challenge the "All you can drink" offer. But the fact remains, whether you consume three drinks or thirty (and that's been done), you get the same tab — just $10.95.

Holidays at the 'Boat are somethin' special. "Thanksgiving on the River" signifies a Turkey Day of Dining, Dancing, and Entertainment for the whole family — Traditional Holiday Dinner — 2 Bands — and a Show — Free Faberge for Mom — Gifts for the kids. First child eats free all day and parents can buy a Turkey Feast for just $6.95.

Speaking of American Express, they've been sitting on a unique idea for some time. It's particularly appropriate for this holiday period. American Express calls this convenience "Be My Guest" and here's how it works: First requisite is, quite naturally, that you are an American Express card holder. That gives you the privilege of inviting anyone you wish to dine at any American Express Member Establishment Restaurant. You needn't be present. This bill will be charged to your account. Call American Express' New York Telephone Service Center 677-1111 or 677-5500 and ask for "Be My Guest." And you thought American Express only related to Traveler's Checks!

Irascible Toots Shor, the last of the great saloon keepers, has gotta get the award for "comeback of the year" — Out of action less than two years ago, Toots opened a joint opposite the Garden on 33rd St. last year and he has flourished mightily. Toots' legion of friends flocked to the place on opening day and it seems they never left. Flushed with this success. Toots gave serious thought to opening a second joint on the Eastside. He found a great location opposite the Biltmore on 43rd, where so many of Toots' cronies stay. Toots Shor II opened October one. Toots confided that one of the highlights of his life was realized this spring when George Steinbrenner invited Toots to throw out the first ball at the opening of Yankee Stadium.

Here's a genuine New York Horatio Alger saga. A little over a year ago, a fellow by the name of Dave Rubin, long experienced in handling group travel business, conceived a company he calls "Party Line." The idea was to provide a service for people and groups looking to have a private party whatever the occasion, regardless of size. Dave and Party Line then lined up over 200 of New York's leading restaurants and hotels to participate. The rest is history. Party Line is thriving, and best of all the service is FREE. Call Dave at 563-7450 just in time for Christmas and New Year's.

Address: Nat'l Press Bldg., 27 W. 34th St., New York, N. Y. 10001

Sample tip sheet:

```
FROM:          _____ Restaurant

TO:            Editors of local newspapers
               Food and entertainment columnists
               Local television and radio news
               Entertainment editors

SUBJECT:       Celebrity Night to be held at
               _____ Restaurant in coopera-
               tion with the Health Promotion Drive.

WHO:           Screen star _____, gold cham-
               pion _____, writer _____,
               and other celebrities of the screen,
               sports, and literary worlds will
               attend Celebrity Night.

WHAT:          Celebrity Night at the _____
               Restaurant will be held to mark the
               cooperation between figures of the
               screen, sprots, and literary worlds
               in the newly organized Health Promo-
               tion Drive, which is designed to
               collect funds for promoting health,
               research, and development on all
               fronts.

WHY:           While certain phases of health promo-
               tion have received contributions --
               in many cases far more generous for
               their development programs than
               anticipated -- other phases have been
               underfinanced. Celebrity Night is the
               kick-off of a campaign to provide a
               better balance in the financial
               support of efforts to solve existing
               problems.

WHEN:          (Date and time)

WHERE:         _____ Restaurant (Banquet Room)

               Your representation is cordially requested.

                           Sincerely yours,


For further information,
CONTACT:       (Your name)
               (Your telephone number)
```

Sample press release:

FOR RELEASE ON (Date)

(Name) RESTAURANT CATERERS YMCA

BOARD OF DIRECTORS DINNER

The annual Board of Directors
dinner of the _____
YMCA will be held tomorrow
evening at (time) P.M. at
_____ Restaurant.

According to Stamford Norgate,
YMCA Vice President and Secretary, announcement of plans for
the construction of a new YMCA
building will be made by the
organization's President,
Richard Hemingway.

The dinner, which will feature
_____ Restaurant's fa-
mous (name of dish), will be
attended by _____'s Mayor
James J. Koster and members of
the City Council, as well as by
YMCA directors.

CONTACT: (Your Name)
           (Your Telephone Number)

Sample press release:

FOR RELEASE ON (Date)

_____ RESTAURANT
TO SPONSOR CHRISTMAS PARTY
FOR UNDERPRIVILEGED CHILDREN

A Christmas party for
underprivileged children,
to be held in the recrea-
tion room of the downtown
YMCA, will be sponsored
by _____ Restaurant,
the fast-food eatery known
for its hamburgers, pizzas,
and southern fried chicken.

The party, which will
be held on Monday, December
___, will feature entertain-
ment by Bozo, the Magician,
The Loops, a rock dancing
and singing trio, and a
western movie.

Food for the party,
supplied by the restaurant,
will be prepared by two of
the establishment's regular
chefs on portable stoves and
other equipment supplied by
_____'s.

Each guest will also
receive a gift-wrapped
present and other favors.

CONTACT: (Your name)
           (Your telephone
            number)

speaker was than they will be in a release which states, "Horizon's new banquet hall opens tomorrow" and goes on to describe decor, service features, and food selection, which are more appropriate for an advertisement than for a publicity release.

PUBLIC RELATIONS: WHAT IS IT?

According to Dr. R. W. McIntosh, sales promotion and merchandising authority, public relations can be defined as "an attitude of management which places first priority on the public interest when making management decisions."

Webster's *New Collegiate Dictionary* defines public relations as, "The activities of an organization in building and maintaining sound and productive relations with special publics, such as customers, employees, and the public at large."

To put it in the simplest terms, public relations is *anything* that you, your restaurant, or any representative does that influences your image in the eyes of the public; anything that distinguishes you from your competitor.

Public relations can be positive or negative. If one waiter is insolent, or if his apparel is soiled or baggy, that's negative public relations. If the condition of the restrooms is clean and luxurious, that constitutes positive public relations.

Public relations themes differ from one restaurant to another. However, most people agree that there is no industry in which a favorable public attitude towards the entrepreneur is more important to success than the restaurant industry. And while *Friendly's* conveys the public relations image of quality, while *McDonald's,* that of fun, each has an important responsibility to maintain the very best image possible.

Public relations differs from publicity in this respect: Publicity usually comprises *nonpaid* submissions to various outside media such as newspapers, radio, and television. Public relations, on the other hand, is aimed at personal exposure in the community and involves activities that are often paid for and designed to bring a business or person in contact with the public in a favorable light.

The kind of public relations you do will depend only in part of the kind of restaurant you run (self service, fast food, ethnic identity, hotel, night club, etc.). Naturally, each category has particular characteristics that the public expects to find when it goes to eat there. Basically, however, no matter what kind of establishment you run, your growth and success depend upon the food quality and preparation, service, efficiency, and friendliness, convenience of location, cost of food as compared with your competition, and featured dishes, including ethnic variety, entertainment, and purchasing advantages.

COMMUNITY PARTICIPATION

As a restaurateur, you have the constant challenge of getting to the top ahead of your competitor and staying there. One requisite for accomplishing this is to expand your perspective. Look beyond your restaurant and your individual customer. Think "community." The entire community is your market. Involve yourself. Play an active role in social, civic, and charity events. Show that you are concerned about public welfare. Valuable public relations, community appreciation, and good will are thus achieved.

COURTESY CALLS ON INFLUENTIAL MEMBERS IN THE COMMUNITY

It's always helpful to drop in on influential members of the community—to become acquainted with them and to learn about their problems, particularly if your services may help to solve some of them. You may even be able to offer some of those services as a matter of good will.

For instance, why not offer various city officials—the mayor, members of legislative bodies (particularly representatives of your district), the police commissioner—free use of your banquet rooms for special meetings? Or inform the Chamber of Commerce that you would be delighted to cooperate in its activities.

In most communities there are numerous local organizations involved in some phase of public benefits that are more than happy to accept any contribution or cooperation you may be able to give. If you do give, you can feel confident that your cooperation will be returned by the officials and organization representatives with whom you become acquainted through 1) their own patronage, and 2) their recommendations of your restaurant to other organizations and individuals.

Business firms can also be public relations factors in building both your clientele and the success of your establishment. Get to know the executives of such firms. Learn what you can do for them. By helping them, you will also enlist their help in building your restaurant patronage.

Even if you are unable to enlist the help of business executives, their secretaries or telephone operators in city departments, organization offices, and business firms can be very helpful patronage builders. You will be amazed how much promotion such individuals can do for your establishment in return for a complimentary meal or a reduced rate coupon. Often, they'll be willing to distribute your card or other material to fellow employees, and may even permit you to place a small notice on their switchboard or bulletin board.

One midwestern restaurant achieves the help and gratitude of receptionists and other "business-recommenders" by sending them a Valentine's Day gift of a complimentary meal certificate.

BE A JOINER

In smaller communities particularly, becoming a "joiner" in civic, charitable, and other public organizations can be a most influential public relations tool for a dining establishment. Such organizations often hold events which can be most profitable to you, especially if you have private rooms where you hold meetings, dances, and other affairs. Remember that your membership in such organizations also achieves valuable individual contacts and potential patronage.

PARTICIPATE IN COMMUNITY ACTIVITIES

Your participation in community activities as a member of block associations, as a committee member helping to organize parades, raise funds for charities, support projects for community improvement, and participate in public events also helps to build your restaurant's reputation and image.

PARTICIPATE IN WORTHWHILE CAUSES

Is your community seeking to build a new hospital? A school? A playground? Is the Heart Fund, the Cancer Society, or some other health research organization holding its annual campaign? Become active in as many such projects as possible. In all such projects, you will find new friends, new associates, and, most important to you, of course, new customers and sources of potential customers.

HONOR GUESTS WITH SPECIAL EVENTS

Try to find out the dates of birthdays, anniversaries, and other noteworthy events in the lives of your customers and their families. You can do this by placing a "Special Events Date Card" on each of your tables with each new setting. The card should have space for listing dates for birthdays, anniversaries, and "other special dates." There should also be space on the card for writing in the customer's name and address. You should note these occasions on separate file cards in a "Customer's Event File."

Several weeks in advance of each event, the customer should be contacted by mail and offered a special dinner at a reduced price with prizes, bonuses, and/or appropriate free items such as a birthday cake as inducement to celebrate the event at your establishment.

GIVE A CHRISTMAS PARTY
FOR YOUR BEST CUSTOMERS

Quite a few restaurants today express their appreciation to their best customers by holding a Christmas party during the holiday season. Usually, they mail invitations with a reply card enclosed, inviting the customer and his family to attend. A reply card asks the customer to list the names of the family members who will attend and the ages of any children. The party generally includes both food and entertainment such as music and dancing for the adults, or a magician for the children. Special favors, each with a gift card that has the recipient's name, are placed on the table of attending family.

OFFER TEAM AND GROUP SPONSORSHIPS

Business establishments sometimes sponsor athletics or group events that are designed to develop the community's youth or to build the community's image. Such support often leads to the sponsor's name being embroidered on the uniforms of the team involved and/or in special billboards, articles, and other notices in the event's programs. These notices, in addition to offering the appreciation of the organizers and participants, can also serve to publicize its sponsors, especially those in the restaurant field.

The *Mel Markin* restaurant in Chicago, for example, is only one of a number of restaurants that has sponsored a girls' baseball team. As a result of their help, they reaped good public relations exposure in their respective communities.

PERSONNEL AS A PUBLIC RELATIONS FACTOR TO CONSIDER

Remember that your personnel carries your name and your image. How they look and act has a definite impact on your image. To assure effective image and public relations, Sky Chef provides 25 separate areas of observation for a manager to consider in his personnel's relationship with the public. Sky Chef's personnel are graded on the basis of uniform neatness, manner of greeting guests, and general, overall attitude. This is not only a part of the initial training, but a continuing means of maintaining close quality control over personnel.

The feeling of well-being, supported by a good and growing reputation and a mutually satisfying relationship between management and staff, is the heart of a sound public relations program. Any restaurant owner must create a harmonious atmosphere among the employees within his operation. The staff must all work together to satisfy the public's desire for good food and service.

Knowing how to do this starts with an effort and awareness on the part of the management. It is up to management to make the public aware of consistently courteous service. This should be reinforced through the behavior and attitude of every member of the staff, from the waiters to the busboys.

MAILINGS/FLYERS

Perhaps you can manage to post one of your menus on the bulletin boards of various firms. You can follow this up with a mailing to the company executives—a well-designed card, for instance. You can also write a form letter, reproducing it so that it looks as personal as possible, announcing a policy of executive luncheon specials. You might want to make a point of emphasizing foods that are low in cholesterol. Or that you are featuring a national cuisine. Your letter could begin by saying, "We've taken a leaf from the great restaurants of Milan, the business center of Italy, and added (a North Italian regional dish) for our business clientele."

If your luncheon special isn't directed to any one particular business group, insert flyers under windshield wipers in the company's parking lot. You can emphasize your quick service by offering a free dessert if the luncheon takes longer than an hour.

THE GRAND OPENING

A Grand Opening is the culmination of many promotional steps making the community aware of you. The spotlight and flags tell passing traffic that something big is happening. But you want as many people as possible to anticipate the event and to come with their friends to make your opening a happy, crowded occasion. (For further details, See Chapter 7.)

THE "HUMAN TOUCH"

• Offer long-term employees stock in your restaurant. This is a good news story for your local newspaper or a trade magazine. You can also give theater or film tickets to the waiter whose monthly checks total the biggest amount. Encourage employee involvement by giving cash prizes to employees for the best suggestion on improving service, promotion, or decor.

• Establish a continuing relationship with hotel directors so that you will be informed of conventions coming to town. Write to the organizations and ask if you can advertise in a special publication they might be printing.

- About a week before Thanksgiving, hold a drawing for a free turkey—cooked at your restaurant.
- Distribute free pumpkin seeds to children. Later, at harvest time, hold a contest for the largest one and give the owner a prize.
- Share your anniversary. Bake a huge cake with a dime, a thimble, a wedding ring or other small items baked into it. Customers finding the items in their cake get a free meal.
- Award a prize—perhaps a twenty-five dollar Government bond—to the first baby born at your local hospital each month.
- Hold a flower arranging contest. Display the top winning entries on tables in your restaurant, with a free meal or cash for the winners.
- Market your renowned salad dressing or cheesecake through your own restaurant and through distributors in other localities.

LOCAL TIE-INS AND GIVE-AWAYS

A great deal of publicity and advertising can be built by setting up special tie-in offers and give-aways. Generally speaking, the tie-ins and give-aways should consist of either a free bottle of wine with dinner, or a free dinner for two with wine.

Effective ways to promote such tie-ins include:

1. Retail shops who offer a free dinner at your restaurant with the purchase of a certain amount of merchandise. You might also consider tie-ins with a local movie house or sports stadium.
2. Radio station advertising as give-aways for contests and promotional programs.
3. Deals with banks, insurance companies, and other financial institutions.

Retail Tie-Ins

Retailers, as well as theater or sports managers, can often be approached very successfully for tie-in deals. For example, a men's clothing store dealing in better quality clothes could be approached on this basis: that you will give a free dinner for two with every purchase of a suit or coat. Of course, you will have to make an equitable and profitable financial arrangement with the store. The store should handle the advertising and promotion of this program.

Radio Advertising

Local radio stations often offer prizes in conjunction with their own advertising and sales promotion programs. In return for free dinners, you can often arrange valuable free publicity and advertising on the local radio stations. Much of this advertising is extremely effective as an advance sales builder. Similar tie-ins can also be made with your local television stations. Much of the advantage of the television advertising, of course, is that you may get some graphic representation of your restaurant on the TV screens. This type of advertising is enormously valuable in building business.

Financial Institutions

The third opportunity to use a tie-in free dinner offer is with banks. The offer here has the slight variation from that of the retail merchandise offering, since some banks are limited by local statutes regarding the amount of money they can spend for prizes with opening accounts. You might possibly have to make some adjustment in your offer to comply with these laws. The value of bank advertising for your restaurant is great, because the association ties you in to the very distinguished image that banks have built for themselves. On the other hand, the banks that tie in to your image can break away from their own stodgy image into a more "with it" appearance that comes along with a more modern and up-to-date business image.

All these free dinner offers should be tied directly to advertising programs that carry across the idea of wonderful, distinctive dining in your restaurant. Ad headlines could be something like:

"Buy a new suit and have dinner on us."

"Celebrate your new bank account as our guest for dinner at (your restaurant)."

"Your local Oldsmobile dealer wants you to be his guest for dinner."

If you have a snack bar near a bowling alley or tennis court, set up portable snack tables and serve a light salad as well as a variety of fruit juices, sodas, and beer. Advertise a free lunch to the winners of important tournaments. Your connection with sports and athletic events can imply health—a campaign you can use in your media advertising: "We've learned a lot catering to the appetites of East Village's tennis players. Physical fitness is our concern, too. Drop by and try our fresh salads."

Raffles and Coupons

Another gambit for slack periods is a raffle or drawing of all customers' checks during a certain period of time. The customer should keep a receipt, and the one whose bill is picked gets either a refund on his meal or another equivalent meal free. The more expensive the meal, the greater the freebee, and the more incentive the customer has to order more. Or, you can lure new customers with coupon specials. Print coupons on your newspaper ads as well as on take-out boxes. When the customer returns with ten coupons, give him a free pizza, ice cream cone, or cookie.

PROMOTE YOUR FOOD ITEMS

Advertise Specialities

If you serve specialty foods that can be taken home, advertise them with a sign in the window. If your premises are large enough, set aside a small area for a take-out department to the side of the front entrance. This can be done in any restaurant, no matter what your price level, nor whether your specialty is fishcakes and root beer or prime meat and quiche Lorraine.

Advertise specials that appeal to the tastes of various groups in your community. Soup or juice, a sandwich, dessert, and coffee can be offered as a special to business people. Or combine one of your specialties with an appetizer and coffee, shave a little off the total price, and tag it your "executive specialty."

Let the world know you serve something besides hamburgers or steak and potatoes. If your cuisine is specialized, advertise it. Ethnic foods have become increasingly important to Americans. If a large part of your community has foreign roots, it's a good idea to introduce ethnic dishes into your menu. These foods can be adapted for an opulent, expensive menu or for fast foods.

If you serve sandwiches, you know that they no longer mean white bread only. They can be served on Italian or French bread, a bagel, or a pita, a round flat, Middle Eastern bread that opens like a pocket and is an excellent substitute for more familiar breads.

If you serve homemade specialties—made either at your restaurant or by a local person—advertise it. Become famous for your soups or pastries or ice cream. Homemade items usually prepared off the premises by a baking company, for instance, are always impressive items, particularly for prospective diners who know nothing about your restaurant. The word "homemade" says you take pride in your food.

Weekly specialties allow the restaurateur to experiment with various new dishes without creating serious distractions or overburdening the kitchen. You can schedule ahead for such meals, even meals that may be complex and innovative. They also give adventuresome eaters new foods to try. Run a newspaper ad describing the specialty, whether it be moussaka or a new flavored ice cream. Try to publicize it with a tempting photograph.

Ice cream in particular is a favorite food in the take-out and gourmet categories, especially when it is homemade with all natural ingredients. Americans are mad about ice cream, and even madder for the infinite variety of flavors it so often comes in. If it is rich and creamy enough, and the flavors crazy enough, you can have lines trailing outside your store even during the winter months. While you may not want to crowd the store with machinery as well, ice cream machines are nevertheless an eye-catching device and often help to build trade.

PUBLIC RELATIONS RECIPROCITY

If your restaurant is one of a chain, offer some promotion for the others nearby. Have a list of the sister franchises in the vicinity on your cashier's desk. Let the other franchise holders know of your referral and ask them to reciprocate.

DISCOUNTS

You can often attract people who work nearby by offering a discount. The reduction can be permanent or temporary to attract first-time customers or to introduce a new product: "With our new crunchy doughnuts, you get a cup of coffee FREE." One Toledo restaurant increased business enormously by offering a $1.00 discount on take-out purchases over a certain amount.

COURT THE BUSINESS COMMUNITY

While many of the snack bars and restaurants in your business district may close early, business meetings often go on long after 5 o'clock. Advertise your hours, printing them on a small card and enclosing a menu. Send the mailing around to receptionists at different firms and government agencies. If there are employees you know who can be particularly helpful in bringing in additional business, invite them in for a free meal to sample your food.

FREEBEES AND CONTESTS

At Christmas time, one well-known Chicago restaurant sent a thank you letter to their most frequent and most important customers, expressing appreciation for their patronage. The letter also told them that a gift was being reserved in their name, which they would receive upon receipt of the letter after their next meal. The gift was useful and inexpensive—a pair of salad servers or a popular book or some novelty that could be bought in quantity at a discount. A variation of this is a free dessert on presentation of your invitational mailer. This can also be used as an introductory lure to business employees.

Invite people to try their luck and your food at the same time. Offer a valuable prize encased in a box. After dinner, offer each patron a possible key to that box. The person with the right key gets the contents—a savings bond, perhaps, or a $25 gift certificate to a local store. The gift should be appropriate for both men and women.

If your clientele is young, be sure it's also suitable to their age bracket.

The perennial Guess the Beans (or Marbles or Pennies) in the Jar game still has fascination. The prize to the person who guesses correctly can be a free meal (set a price limit). The guessing game can be open either to the general public or to customers only.

A NEW MANAGEMENT? PUBLICIZE IT

If you have taken over the premises of a restaurant with a reputation for brusque, inefficient service, bad or uneven food quality, or high prices, you might have to work hard at regaining customers.

In this case, you might want to convey a highly personal image so that the public thinks of you more as a host than as a restaurant owner. Hold an open house for patrons of the restaurant that preceded yours. If you're fortunate enough to inherit a mailing list, use it. Otherwise, you can give them invitations when they dine at your establishment. That mailing list can also be used to invite regular customers to pick up an attractive gift waiting for them at some particular time after you have built up a following.

A radical change of menu is one important way to tell people that the restaurant is under new ownership. It also conveys the impression of a management that can change and keep up with the times. This new menu can be helpful in several ways. Many restaurants, for example, get around inflation by offering a small number of entrees and by keeping the food simple, thus reducing labor costs. However, customers get unadorned high quality food.

Instead of tasteless, frozen vegetables, try serving crisp salad with a variety of dressings along with bowls of bacon bits and croutons. Customers can mix their own salad at a buffet and eat as much of it as they want. Dieters will love you, and you can offer their nondieting friends hors d'oeuvres and dessert.

Bringing the kitchen into the dining room is another way to make your restaurant and its ownership distinctive. For example, customers love to watch the pizza chef throwing and twirling the dough before it is piled with cheese and tomatoes. And even in more formal restaurants customers love to watch the final touches on a flambee or sizzling rice dish. You can set up a grill in the rear, sectioned off with bare bricks and presided over by a chef in a traditional tall white hat and apron.

When you do this, you allow the audience to see more than simply a good show. You are also inviting your customers to watch the food making process, a display that implies integrity. You are implying that your kitchen is clean enough to be up front.

ENCOURAGE NEIGHBORHOOD YOUTHS

If you have an operation with a luncheon counter or soda fountain, the "Happy Hour" approach can be adapted for school children who rush off to their neighborhood soda fountain after school. Serve cookies or ice cream at half price one day a week from three to four P.M., advertising this special with a sign in the window. Other promotions you might try are listed below.

- Try comic strip advertising in your local newspaper.

- Pile ice cream cones in a transparent plastic container in your window. The child who guesses the number of cones most accurately gets free ice cream for a week.

- Turn your soda fountain into a Saturday night "must" for teenagers by permitting dancing to jukebox music. Parents who spend the weekends wondering where their children are will be eternally grateful.

- Don't overlook the business possibilities of catering to young appetites. What about becoming a concessionaire at basketball, football, and other sporting events? Make an appointment to visit the school principal or another administrator in charge.

- Give away free passes to a children's Saturday movie matinee on their birthday.

- Advertise on a bulletin board in your local high school.

PROMOTIONS AIMED AT CHILDREN

In considering children, as well, professional advice can be a help. Emmanuel Winston of Winston Gray, Inc., a premium manufacturing and merchandising company, for example, says that "the toy should have action," because this stimulates the child's imagination and lends itself to supportive advertising, particularly television." Winston also believes that toys should give children a sense of accomplishment even if they can't manipulate it well at first.

"Go for the biggest toy you can afford," he advises. "Offer something specific. 'Toy' is nowhere near as powerful an image builder as 'fire truck' or 'frisbee.' "

Many of these imaginative promotions directed at children bring in adult business along with the kids. Rag dolls, for example, are a great favorite among the kids: The Ronald McDonald and the Hamburglar dolls from McDonald's, the Burger King doll, and the Gilbert Giddy-Up doll from Hardee's are tremendously popular. The International House of Pancakes offered miniature reproductions of National Football League helmets, and Bumbleberry sold a "giggle stick," with twirling plastic rings that change direction when they are rubbed with another stick.

Children's give-aways are also a successful way of attracting business and can be fun and imaginative as well. Purchasers of 16-ounce drinks from Tastee Freeze, for example, got a "monster cup." Burger Chef has packaged burgers in gaily decorated boxes that are accompanied with a surprise toy—a dune buggy, a whistle train, crayons and a stencil, a flying saucer.

PROMOTIONAL ADVICE

Jack Seidman, President of Spot O' Gold, Inc., found that "any successful promotion requires that the employees be knowledgeable about the offer. [It] takes about two weeks to get started. In the next three or four weeks, tremendous interest is generated by the media and word of mouth. After the seventh week, you should stop advertising it and allow another two weeks for the promotion to drift out.*

DO'S AND DON'T'S: MORE IDEAS

- Do advertise premiums by banners outside the store.
- Don't run one promotion into another. Let several weeks elapse before moving on to another one, the experts counsel.

---

* From the April, 1973 issue of *Fast Foods*.

- Tee shirts are popular all over the country. Why not have your restaurant's name and logo imprinted on them, and sell them for a modest fee? Remember that it's free advertising for you.

- You might also be interested in the fact that the greatest amount of time and money in promotions is spent on the young. Eighty percent of all promotions are directed toward them.

- The biggest promotion category for adults is glassware. How about considering a personalized coffee mug or dessert dish?

- Offer a commission to a local civic organization with a fund raising program for all member referrals and purchases, and/or a discount to all group members or party groups.

- Take a big step beyond a take-out service: Go into mail order. Advertise in publications you feel will pull the best for you. (You will, of course, have to choose foods that will stay fresh.)

- Get a list of newcomers to the area and send them a welcoming letter. Offer a special discount or a gift as a get-acquainted feature.

- List your restaurant in the telephone yellow pages of other communities.

- Make your delivery truck colorful. Paint your name in large letters and add your symbol on the top or sides.

- Banks sometimes have community exhibits. Co-sponsor one with the bank—an exhibit of crafts by the elderly, perhaps, or paintings by children. Maybe someone has cleaned out his attic and found a fortune in antiques. Arrange an "Our Town in 1880" show. Consider these public relations gestures.

- Another intriguing, attention-getting idea is to insert a portion of a picture—e.g. an illustration of your restaurant—within a sealed envelope. Each customer gets one with each meal. When the accumulated pieces form a complete picture, a prize is given. The names of the winners are subsequently posted in the restaurant.

- If you send a mailing to your clientele, show your interest in their reactions and feelings by enclosing a checklist on which they can rate food quality, service, ambience, and menu offers. (Are there any dishes they would like added to the menu?)

- Sponsor a baking contest at a local fair. The winner should be chosen by a local notable and should receive an order from you for several cakes.

- Direct your attention to any remodeling you do by running a contest for the best art painted on the temporary wall structure. You'll have a colorful mural on the face of your building until the new front is ready for an unveiling.

- Sponsor a local fishing contest, giving the catcher of the largest fish first prize: dinner for two.

- Hold a children's ad contest for children under eighteen. The person who writes the best copy not only gets his work and his name published in the local paper, but gets a special, personalized, homemade cake.

- Announce special foreign menus or wine tasting events on picture postcards depicting a French vineyard, say, or a couple dining in a scenic place like Capri, and send it to your clientele.

- Reprint a newspaper ad on tinted stock and send copies to people on your mailing list.

- Gather your staff around you and take a homey photograph for your Christmas and New Year's mailing.

- Arrange a tie-in with a local store and offer customers a half-price lunch on presentation of a card they receive with their purchase. You can split the cost of the lunch with the store owner.

REAL-LIFE EXAMPLES
OF PUBLIC RELATIONS CAMPAIGNS

Below are some examples of public relations campaigns that actual restaurants conducted with great success.

Gino's 300 units gave away 15,000 scouting leader kits a month (this came to about 50 per month per store) for three years.

Taylor's restaurant, in Tustin, California, achieved favorable public relations by passing out 1,000 pots of coffee to motorists waiting in line at a nearby service station during the gas shortage. So did a *Hardee's* unit in Charlotte, North Carolina. Both stores reaped valuable dividends in added patronage from grateful motorists.

Don Roth's Blackhawk offers a "show shuttle" for dinner guests, transporting them to theater and sporting events. It also provides a "brunch bus" to the Bears' football game.

Mel Markon's in Chicago offers "Annual Thanks" for patronage and appreciation in the form of two lunches for the price of one.

Piqueo in Chicago caters to the family. It invites patrons to call in advance to order what they want (duck, lamb, goat, etc.), so all foods served are based on patron requests. The proprietor says, "My family treats people as if they're our guests. Everyone brings new people back, so we don't even have to advertise."

Mama Lena, also in Chicago, builds good public relations by talking to hotel bell captains and offering free dinners for new business.

Gage & Tollner in Brooklyn, N.Y., gave free subway tokens to its patrons. These served the dual function of luring patrons from Manhattan and of building good public relations.

Sage's East in Chicago extracted some humor from Watergate and added it to the drinks. In a notice to customers, the owner asked that no one take offense "at this gesture, which allows us to laugh at ourselves even through our tears, a typically American characteristic." Sage served such specials as the "Deep Throat Tequilla," ("One sip and only the Washington Post will know your identity"); the "Sirica Stinger," ("Gives you no immunity"); and the "Old Fashioned Impeachment."

Arnie's in Chicago is owned by a veteran of the Playboy empire. Arnold Morton has placed pieces from his own art collection around the restaurant, adding to its mirrored pillars, sophisticated cuisine, and glowing chandeliers. Different rooms vary in mood and style, from avant-garde in the main lounge, to upholstered elegance in the main dining room, to a cultivated outdoorsiness in the garden room.

Morton's first employees were college students and actors who won a reputation for friendliness. His entire operation blended into his goal: "A large operation . . . on a personalized basis."

Allgauer's Fireside Restaurant also in Chicago threw a "tasting luncheon" for food editors. Blindfolded, guests had to identify sample entrees through taste only. Blindfolds were taken off for a dessert flambee.

Decor can strongly influence sales. One restaurant in San Jose, California put a circular table around a hearth. This conveyed the idea and the actuality of a warm center within the surrounding, sleek decor.

Cooky's Steakpub in New York ran an ad listing its entrees and its prices. This included a special $1.00 price for children under 12 Sunday through Friday and a free drink.

Arby's roast beef restaurants in Ohio offered a colorful coffee mug to all customers who bought a roast beef sandwich. The mugs cost anywhere from ten to thirty-five cents, depending on the store's location.

The best promotions have included a "freebee" in which customers who buy a drink can keep the glass.

A professional promotion takes planning and follow-through. Many are created by teams of advertising, design, and psychology experts. If you have the time and money, you would probably benefit from the use of a professional consultant who can give you the very best advice on what will hold a person's attention and interest.

Chapter 7

Grand Opening Promotion Plans

Your restaurant opening is both an opportunity and a responsibility. An opportunity to promote and publicize your restaurant with great festival-like fanfare. A responsibility to present yourself to your public in the most favorable way possible. If you succeed, your clientele will not only try you; they'll also come back. If you don't, they'll stay away themselves and probably also tell their friends to stay away, too.

The Grand Opening of a restaurant is similar to a Broadway play. Without proper and adequate rehearsal and out-of-town try-outs, the Grand Opening will be a failure. Even if everyone performs as directed, the critics may still pan the play. For you, it's vital that you make sure you're ready for the Grand Opening prior to its commencement. Strive to hold it on the actual day of your opening, and not earlier. Wait several days, weeks, or even months until you are absolutely certain that you're operating smoothly.

PREOPENING AND GRAND OPENING PUBLICITY

The restaurant just starting out will need certain selling tools to acquaint its community of its existence and induce people to try it out. It cannot afford to depend upon traffic alone, unless it occupies an ideal location. There are certain basic items that comprise pre-opening and Grand Opening promotions and publicity.

Since publicity is of prime importance in Grand Opening events, these items should be planned and executed with the utmost care and thought. Most media need local news for their coverage. They will give you such coverage if your news is of interest to their audience. Thus good planning can also result in free advertising.

Good planning means careful timing. Six weeks prior to the Grand Opening, the leading newspapers and television and radio stations that have public interest columns or interview shows should be contacted personally and advised of the plans for the Grand Opening.

Radio spots in particular are useful, since the cost of airing a spot can be relatively low, while the audience you reach can be both specific and quite large. Try using 20-second announcement spots on popular programs three days prior to the opening. These should then be aired daily during the opening period.

At the same time, a press release should be sent to media people. This should include the events planned for the opening, a description of your restaurant, and a sample menu.

A photographer should be hired for any preopening and opening celebrations to take photos of important visitors with the restaurant owner. If the press does not cover the opening, he should take glossy photos. These, along with captions and a release covering the opening, should be sent to the press, television, and radio the next day. Display your best photos in your window.

Other publicity "musts" include the following.

1. Signs should be made by a local sign painter and placed in store windows, announcing the impending opening of your restaurant.

2. About one or two weeks prior to the opening, as soon as a firm Grand Opening date is established, signs should be placed in the window announcing the date, as well as advertising door prizes, specials, give-aways, and "twofers." Celebrities attending the opening should be highlighted.

3. Five days prior to the Grand Opening, an ad should be placed in local newspapers announcing the forthcoming opening. This ad, usually of moderate size, should state the location of the restaurant and the opening date.

Suggested promotion timetable and check list for grand opening.

Approximate Date	Fill in Date	
Six weeks prior to Grand Opening		•Begin search for store promotion and display props. •Order store front "Coming Soon" sign. •Compile mailing list for invitations to preview party and Grand Opening.
Four to five weeks before Opening		•Home office training period.
Three weeks before Opening		•Send material for preopening handbill and door prize stubs to the printer. •Contact newspapers and radio stations and advise them of your program. Reserve time and space in advance. •Get signs for promotion wagon painted. •Obtain list of city and local leaders. •Send our Grand Opening press release #1.

Two to three weeks before Grand Opening		•Send radio commercials to stations confirming broadcast dates and times and the order in which commercials are to run.
		
		•Arrange for radio time spots: Spot #1 to run during week before opening; Spot #2 to run during week of opening.
		
		•Send material for preopening ad, Grand Opening ad, and post-opening ad to newspapers, confirming running dates and position requested.
		
		   •Ad #1 to run one week prior to opening.
		
		   •Ad #2 to run the day before opening.
		
		   •Ad #3 to run the day of the opening.

Approximate Time	Fill in Date	
Two to three weeks before Opening		• Mail out invitations ten to fourteen days prior to opening. • Meet with group that will man the pre-opening promotion vehicle and be certain that everything is ready and in order.
Eleven to fourteen days before Opening		• • Arrange for music, live or canned. • Arrange for photographer to take shots of the exterior and the interior with personnel prior to the preview party, and during the party, the Grand Opening parade, and the festivities. • Have door prize ballot box made. • Acquire any exterior promotion materials required, such as signs, flags, etc.
Ten days before Opening		• Have an informal opening of the restaurant. • Change top panel of window sign. Cover the "Opening Soon" sign with a "Now Open" one.
Nine days before Opening		• Check on all materials required, including paper cups, give-away menus, guest and promotion prizes, door prize stubs, ballot boxes, and ribbons that will be cut during the inauguration ceremony.
Seven days before Opening		• Send out Grand Opening press release #2. • Start running newspaper ad series #1. • Start running radio spot #1.
Three to six days before Opening		• Rehearse preview party and Grand Opening with people who will be involved with the conduct of the parties. • Reminder calls to important guests and editors.
Two days before Opening		• Set up promotion materials for the preview party.
One day before Opening		• Newspaper ad #2 should run. • Preview party should be held.

Approximate Time	Fill in Date	
One day before Grand Opening		· Clean up after preview party and start setting up for Grand Opening. · Decorate exterior of restaurant.
GRAND OPENING DAY		· Make notes on preview party to include in press release. · Finish preparations early and make final inspection. Check for props and sure equipment is functioning. · Grand Opening ceremony for the public. Circulate, meet as many people as possible, get signatures in the guest book, create the impression that the owner is a friendly person and that the Mr. Dunderbak Shop is a fun place. · Make notes for the press release. · Start running Radio Spot #2.
The day after Grand Opening		· Newspaper ad #3 should run. . Send press release #3 covering preview party and Grand Opening to the press, TV, and radio columnists (by hand). · Promotion team with or without promotion vehicle begins handing out handbills for the remainder of the promotion period.
Post Opening		· Announcement on last day of opening period of winner of the Grand Door Prize. Post the person's name in the window. Notify the winner with a telephone call or letter. · Daily door prizes, if offered, should be selected each night. The drawing should continue until a winner is present, if presence is required for the prize. · Collect all the publicity notices and photographs resulting from the pre-opening and opening periods and prepare a continuing press scrap-book. · Develop a live mailing list from the signitures in the guest book.

4. The day before the Grand Opening, the restaurant should be decorated with Grand Opening banners and pennants.

5. On the day of the Grand Opening a newspaper ad two or three times the size of the first announcement should feature several specials.

6. Local school students might be employed to give out flyers in and around the restaurants during the opening week.

GRAND OPENING PROMOTIONS

Sales promotion activities depend upon the time of year, the availability of personnel who can implement the program, and various local events and conditions.

SUGGESTED EVENTS

Many Grand Opening programs include the following events.

1. A preview party for women's club leaders and various city and local officials on the evening before the public opening. Admission should be by invitation only.

2. Grand Opening day should be open to the public. Most openings have invited local personalities and press for publicity.

3. On the Grand Opening day, there are various contests, ceremonies, sales, and entertainment events at the restaurant.

Preview Party for Community Leaders

If you hold such an event, invited guests should include local Women's Club officers, various city and church officials, and other local dignitaries. Contact these officials in writing six weeks prior to the opening. Send another invitation to those you haven't heard from two weeks later, and call any guests who still haven't responded a week before the event.

Once you know your guest list and are prepared for the party, place a guest book near the door for people to sign. This will be the source of a live mailing list. The atmosphere should be festive, and you should either play music on a portable hi-fi or acquire local talent for entertainment.

Suggested wording for various letters of invitation will be found on following pages as well as a suggested Grand Opening time-table on pp. 119–121. Consult this timetable for approximate times to send these out.

Public Grand Opening Day Ceremonies

For the Grand Opening day, you should generate an atmosphere of activity and excitement. Principal guests may be the mayor, local political leaders, business leaders, service club officers, Chamber of Commerce officials, etc. The community's oldest citizen could be one of your honored guests, with an introduction and perhaps an interview about the "good old days."

The Opening Day festivity could be highlighted with free snacks and an inauguration ceremony. Why not start with a dignitary who will cut a ribbon? The restaurant owner can then take possession of the restaurant and serve the first slices of meat to the inaugurating official.

Grand Opening Day Contests

You can conduct various contests, both unique and humorous, to encourage local interest and participation. The Best Costume contest could be handled in fashion show manner, with prizes for all contestants in the form of a credit for a free meal. A "Guess the Number of Peanuts Used in the Restaurant Special Dish" could be another possibility. Or, a token gift can be given to the oldest guests. The restaurant owner should circulate and greet all comers and see that they register in his guest book.

Door Prize Procedure

One customary feature of Grand Opening events is the offering of door prizes. Customers receive a ballot on entering the restaurant; the ballots can also be distributed by the serving people. Drawings are usually made at the end of the period, which is usually at least one week. As many as ten winners might be drawn. Door prize ballots should be printed well in advance. The ballot box for door prizes

Invitation letter to dignitaries.

Dear Mr. _____:

    We will be privileged
to have you as our guest at
our Grand Opening at (hour)
on (date) at the above
address. A number of prominent
citizens of the community are
being invited to acquaint
them with the role we wish
our establishment to play
in the social and economic
life of our community.

    We feel that a service
like ours is a healthy contribution to the community,
since it offers quality food
and quality service.

    We hope that you and
your friends will find time
to join us for an exciting
dining experience.

        Sincerely yours,

Dear Mr. Mayor:

It would be a pleasure to have you as our guest at the Grand Opening of our restaurant on (date and time) at (address).

Invitations are being extended to a select number of prominent people representing the press as well as civic, business, and educational leaders to acquaint them with the role of our restaurant in the community and the contribution we hope to make for the economic health of our area.

Such an enterprise as the _____ Restaurant must by nature be civic-minded. We would be honored if you could find the time to attend our Grand Opening ceremonies.

Would you please let us know if we may expect you?

Thanking you for your consideration,

Sincerely yours,

should be in a prominent location, along with a glass of pencil stubs or pencils on strings nearby. The ballot box could be made out of a square corrugated carton or a lady's hat box covered with colored paper. A simple card announcing the date and time of the drawing should be attached. If you wish to turn this into a raffle, you can offer a drawing ticket to each customer who orders a drink, which they can fill out and stuff in a box for a later drawing.

Daily door prizes should be drawn at a specified hour by a qualified judge selected by the management. If the prize winner is not present, he should either be notified later, or else the drawing should continue until a chosen winner is present.

The Grand Door Prize must be drawn from the total number of door prize stubs there are on the final night of the opening. The name of the winner should be posted in the window.

PERIOD OF CELEBRATION

How long these Grand Opening ceremonies continue will depend upon the time of year and local conditions, such as the size of the community. Many owners feel that they should go on for at least a week. The people use various devices to help keep up the momentum of the opening period, including daily contests, raffles, drawings, or daily door prizes in addition to the grand prize given at the end of the period. Other ongoing promotions may include various introductory sales and discount offers such as "order one and get dessert free" promotions.

In general, Saturday is a good day to begin your Grand Opening celebration. However, local conditions can decide or alter this. Each restaurateur should decide, in light of his own community, the best timing for his opening. Inasmuch as both men and women will frequent your restaurant, you should be particularly careful to hold your opening events while both are available. Be sure to avoid opening at a time when some group is certain to be busy.

PROMOTIONAL VEHICLES

The use of an antique car or some other unusual vehicle to cruise through a town's streets announcing a Grand Opening is often enormously successful publicity. One restaurant that specializes in German foods used a Bavarian beer buckboard. Such vehicles are usually rentable and have signs fixed on each side promoting the store. The vehicle can be used at regular intervals to provide maximum visibility and publicity by driving through various sections of your community.

The driver and passengers can wear costumes, and a public address system should be installed if local ordinances permit. Recorded or live musical numbers can be played, along with announcements and invitations to the opening. Handbills, consisting of the Grand Opening ad printed on inexpensive colored paper, can be handed out to people along the way.

COSTUMES

Unique costumes, attuned to the restaurant or food style, are also effective in attracting attention for Grand Opening occasions. Girls clad in traditional Swiss costumes may celebrate the opening of a Swiss food specialty restaurant. Old-fashioned costumes of the early 1900's can dramatize "Mother's homemade cookin'." You can usually rent these costumes and have teenagers to wear them during the Grand Opening celebration.

TREASURE CHESTS

Try placing a "Treasure Chest" in the restaurant. Give each person who purchases something to eat or drink a key. "Lucky" keys that open the chest win prizes. This entire project can be purchased fairly inexpensively; it costs about $60, including one thousand keys.

Below are further promotional concepts that have been used by restaurants across the nation:

1. *Handbills* to be inserted in windshield wipers of parked autos in nearby industrial parking lots and neighboring streets. These handbills can have a coupon format, presenting an introductory offer.

2. *Sandwich sign* placed on the sidewalk in front of the restaurant. This sign can also be used as a "mobile billboard," carried on the shoulders of an individual who walks

around the neighborhood. The sign should have an attractive, eye-catching illustration and message.

3. *Publicity photographs.* Professional glossy photographs should be taken of the opening day crowd and used for planned publicity and advertising insertions. This is why a photographer should be on hand on opening day.

4. *Preparation of a brochure,* one that folds into business card size, might be distributed around offices and apartment houses in each area. Its theme might be "Meet Your New Neighbor."

5. *Simulation of a telegram.* Have your mailed announcements simulate a telegram, using very large type announcing the opening and any special events to honor the occasion.

6. *Helicopter Advertising.* Drop circulars from a helicopter hovering above the premises. If you decided to number the circulars, you can offer certain lucky numbers coupons that are redeemable for five dollars' worth of food.

Chapter 8

The Added Touches

People dine out not only to satisfy physical hunger, but also to satisfy their desires for luxury, variety, or atmosphere. While the customer, and even the restaurateur, might not be consciously aware of the mood and its components, it is nevertheless an important factor, and a major determinant of whether a restaurant gets repeat patronage or not. This is why the most successful restaurant may not necessarily be the one with the most efficient staff, or even with the best food. People will sometimes pass up better food for an atmosphere of charm and character.

CHARACTER

Take, for instance, *Ratner's,* one of the popular kosher restaurants in New York City, which closed because the neighborhood had drastically changed. While the restaurant was world famous, everything about the operation was plain. The tablecloths were white and slightly worn. The china was white and had a standard no-nonsense thickness. A high ceiling gave a feeling of space, although the tables were closely packed together and increased the lively sound of voices engrossed in conversation. The one luxurious touch in decoration was the showcase filled with strawberry shortcakes and other elaborate pastries. The food was excellent, served simply and in large portions.

But what diners thought gave the restaurant its memorable character most were the waiters. They were known as eccentrics. Quick-witted and irascible old timers who considered themselves gourmets of kosher cuisine, they would grow exasperated when customers didn't take their advice in ordering. And their advice was usually good, because their concern was part of a tradition of personal management and fine food with no frills. Their eccentricity and personal interest made people come back again and again.

FRESH AND ATTRACTIVE FOOD ARRANGEMENTS

The basic and most important ways to dramatize food are through crispness and through arrangements that are pleasing to the eye. Bedraggled parsley can make everything look overcooked. Limp lettuce cannot be hidden by globs of salad dressing. Gravy made for the entree should not run over into the vegetable if both are on the same plate.

CUSTOMER PARTICIPATION IN FOOD PREPARATION

People bored by a production in their own kitchens are fascinated by the expertise of a commercial chef. Why not include a flambeed dish or two on your menu? Or slide beef and other roasts into the view of your customers, who can then decide if the "rare" cut is their kind of rare. Exhibit desserts in a refrigerated showcase. Set up coffee stations throughout the restaurant so that nearby customers can smell the aroma of freshly brewed coffee. Preparing your specialties on stove-tables, before the eyes of your guests (steak and other ingredients are presliced and quickly cooked over a fire in the dining room) is a feature that makes Benianha of Tokyo both famous and successful.

DISHWARE AND ORNAMENTS

Some successful decorative ideas include:

• Freshly ground pepper that can be offered by a waiter bearing an oversized peppermill.

- Small red tabs inserted in a steak to indicate whether the customer has ordered his steak rare, medium, or well-done.

- Use the inedible outer shells of raw fruit to make decorative outer containers. For example, remove watermelon with a small scoop from the shell, making small balls. Then replace the watermelon balls and add an assortment of strawberries and other fresh fruit. Sprinkle with liqueur, add sprigs of mint, and put your natural fresh fruit bowl on the dessert table. Individual fresh fruit salads can be served in scooped-out cantaloupe skins.

- If you use traditional china, you'll probably want a simple, white service that can easily be replaced when dishes break. But fast foods and cafeterias often use paper dishes and plastic utensils that are specially designed to go with the decor. (Plates with ridged dividers that separate parts of the main course with different sauces on them are found in paper but not in china.)

- Plastic cocktail mixers can be designed with the symbol and name of your restaurant on it for take-home advertising. The design can also be used on picks put through sandwiches.

- Invent a utensil to make eating your specialty even more interesting: a miniature two-pronged fork for pork bits or a miniature soup spoon for ice cream.

CANDLELIGHT

Chianti bottles aren't the only bottles that give character to your restaurant and your candles. Use interestingly shaped bottles—different ones on each table—or small dishes or ashtrays. Turn containers which are intended for other purposes into candleholders.

COLOR SCHEME

Stand away from your restaurant and think of it as a piece of sculpture that can be painted. The interior of the dining room is done in blocks of color. The walls and ceiling are midnight blue, a dark but not dull color. Chairs are covered in black and red textured fabric. The carpet is black. Tablecloths and napkins are white. The floor-to-ceiling windows have blue drapes that can be closed, but generally are not, since they frame a view of the city. The only decorations are clear glass bud vases with fresh flowers on the table and original works of art on the walls.

Achieving elegance through color need not be confined to formal and expensive restaurants.

At *Bagels And,* a New York cafeteria, the walls are covered with a decorous chevron pattern. Strips of wood radiate from wood paneled support pillars to the ceiling to create the effect of decorative buttressing.

DECOR: YOUR THEME

Nothing is more interesting than transforming an interior into another place. At *Eat & Drink* in New York City, the humble cafeteria and fast-food place has been improved with an unusual menu (cream cheese and peaches omelet cooked before the customer's eyes, quiche, and homebaked cornbread) and decor, based on the theme of a construction site. The bar is called the Loading Zone and is decorated with lights protected by metal cages—the kind that are used on construction sites. The name of the sandwich bar—"The Sandwich Construction Co."—is announced on a large sign that looks like a handsaw.

At the door customers are handed a tray or a folded carryout lunchbox by an employee in a yellow construction hardhat. Specialties at the counters for sandwiches, salads, main dishes and deli are written on the lids of large paint buckets. Wheelbarrows sit on top of the bar, and shovels are hung all over the place. The construction site theme is eminently suited to the restaurant: It began as part of an enormous construction site, the World Trade Center in New York. Eat & Drink is the creation of Restaurant Associates, the firm that has created unique interiors for both elegant French gourmet restaurants and fast food chains.

In the *Autopub* in New York booths are decorated with the facades of automobiles, both antique and modern. People enter the booth by opening the car door. Customers can choose booths with greater or lesser privacy, depending on which automobile they "enter."

An exotic tropical locale gives the hard-working clientele of *Kona Kai* in Chicago a completely relaxing change of scenery. One of the most thorough-going in carrying out the Polynesian theme, the

Kona Kai's waterfall and stream are surrounded by bamboo work, which makes up everything from the ceiling beams to the thatching and lattice work executed by expert craftspeople. Hand-carved outriggers, ornate cocktail tables, and clam shell light fixtures set off a menu that includes fish and marinated meat dishes in addition to continental dishes.

Celebrate the dining customs and recipes of Tudor England with waiters in jerkins, lights in the form of candles in sconces on the wall, and such specialties as suckling pig and Cockaleekie soup. This is particularly suited to the Christmas season, when the more lyrically inclined on your staff can sing Christmas carols, or when you can hire a singing group that can be decked out in costume as carolers.

Tradition needn't be grafted on. A long-established restaurant comes equipped with its own customs and ambience that should be changed only after careful consideration.

From the speakeasy entrance door to the no-turnover staff, the *Old Barn* in Kentucky has carefully nurtured the accumulation of tradition ever since the restaurant's founding in 1921, despite complete reconstruction and changes in ownership. At one time the restaurant was a private club, which explains the emphasis on developing and retaining the customs and traditions that were tailored to its steady clientele.

Located near an airport, the Old Barn grew in splendor as aviation thrived. But it also takes its character from horse racing, the theme of the original restaurant. The results of the Kentucky Derby are traditionally posted near the entrance of the restaurant by an employee standing by with a radio on the day of the race. The Kentucky Derby theme continues through its main dining room, the Tac Room.

Another dining area, called The Office, began as the office of the original owner. He would serve drinks there to his friends who were waiting to be seated. Maintaining traditions like these is a way of personalizing the act of dining.

Another way the Old Barn does this is by breaking up a large dining area into smaller ones. While you'll want to give a name to each smaller area, you don't have to rush this. Wait until a steady clientele builds up and then ask them for suggestions. Or run a name-the-room contest. Each different area can be differentiated through decorative devices such as color and artwork.

At the *Casa Chez* in Chicago customers pick their own fish, steak, ribs, and chicken and can cook it themselves on outside grills under the supervision of a chef. If this is a new feature in your restaurant, set a special introductory price. Offer two meals for the price of one and a half meals. Or if you run a take-out establishment, offer four sandwiches or meals for the price of three.

Aquariums can double as interior decoration as well as containers from which the customer can choose his own fish. Besides this, he knows his fish is fresh.

Fresh fruit daquiris are a striking way of adding interest to a bar. Keep a variety of soft fruits on hand—peaches, bananas, apricots, mangoes—and allow the customer to make his own choice. Throw it into a blender and mix with brandy, rum, or a daquiri.

NAMES

Food, rooms, waiters—you name it. The last takes cooperation from the waiter, but if your restaurant is the type where customers and staff know each other and develop warm, personal relationships, encourage nicknames for waiters that reflect their characteristics: Butterfly Vic (who should be a six foot, two inch heavyweight), Quiet George (a chatty type), Lucky Jane (who plays the horses).

We've seen how names can be applied to separate, or semi-separate, dining areas. Using the theme of cities, paint murals of Chicago, New York, Houston, Miami, and Atlanta on the walls of various rooms that are named for the city.

Name foods, especially dishes you have created or featured. "Great Gritzbe's Flying Food Show," a mouthful of a name in itself, carries its unique character into the menu. The "French Toast Connection" might combine chicken salad and cheese between slices of French toast. The "Monte Gritzbe" can be a deep-fried ham, turkey, and cheese bread mixture. "Strawberry Fields Forever" might be a dessert room, where customers can get desserts, both hot and cold, for seventy-five cents with a meal, or one dollar twenty-five cents without.

A take-out Chinese restaurant makes its point with its name, the *Chinatown Express*. Such a name can set you apart from others with your versions of even a universal food such as hamburgers. One extra ingredient—a topping of Chinese cooked vegetables, for example— and it becomes an Orientalburger.

Bars are a felicitious place for names and promotions. *Barnaby's*

Family Inn, with company-owned restaurants in the Midwest, origi- nated a Mug Club. Members pay two dollars and get a hand-cast china mug to take home. A membership card allows the member to buy at a discount after eight o'clock, Monday through Friday. A fourteen-ounce stein of Schlitz costs twenty-five cents, and a pitcher, one dollar twenty- five cents, almost half the regular price.

The Plush Horse in Redondo Beach, California, gives double shots from house liquor for one dollar between four and seven P.M. and dubs it "A Bucket for a Buck." Each day the bar highlights an- other drink, named after the day of the week. There's the Merry Mon- day, a Margarita; the Groggy Tuesday, a grog; a Sunny Wednesday, a Tequila Sunrise; a Banger Thursday, a Harvey Wallbanger; a Foggy Friday, a Fogcutter. Drinks of the day are sold at a discount.

If your restaurant is named for a specific place or a specific era, choose names in keeping with the mood. At *Victoria Station,* a coun- trywide chain, a hot drink menu offers drinks named after trains that pulled into London's famous depot. The Irish Mail is Irish coffee; the Flying Scotsman, brandy and hot chocolate; the Glasgo Ltd., hot but- tered rum; Midland & Northern, kahlua coffee; the Golden Arrow, a hot toddy; and the Liverpool & Manchester is a secret formula. The drinks are pegged for a predinner happy hour.

The *Jolly Roger* in California and other western states pegs a pirate theme to its promotions. A black eyepatch, for example, is im- printed on its cocktail glasses.

If you order a corkscrew cocktail at *The Corkscrew Restaurant* in Los Angeles, you'll get a glass of white, red, or rose wine with your dinner.

The "Cappuccino 7" at *Don Roth's Blackhawk* has seven liqueurs "swirled into every sip" of caffe espresso. It also features an Irish Matador with tequila and blended Irish whiskey.

Bon Marche in Chicago has based some of its units on rural Illinois in the 1880's. Blue and white speckled coffee pots, copper skillets, and coffee mugs with farm scenes all carry out this theme. Country dinners are fifty cents less if you are in a party of six or more. Although the food is precooked, vegetables are sliced into irregular shapes to appear homecooked. The total concept is named the "good earth," and includes desserts associated with rural life, such as the Caked Apple Quakenbush, a seven-layer cake with spiced apples and covered with applejack brandy.

SALADS

The infinite variety of salads presents a test of ingenuity and an opportunity for endless promotions. In addition to the standard oil and vinegar, Russian, French and bleu cheese dressings, more can be invented. Name them after your cook, your children, or oceans, and feature a different one every week. Make the salad bar as important as the dessert table. Expand the variety of ingredients customers can choose from. Post possible combinations over the bar. A Blackhawk salad promotion quotes a restaurant critic saying that the ingredients could not be duplicated at home, and emphasizing a particularly delicious dressing: Lorenzo, made with chili sauce, watercress, vinegar, oil, and onions.

EXTERIORS

Even if they want only a hamburger, people are attracted to warmth and character. A sterile exterior says nothing to people passing by who want to relax. The exterior can incorporate traditional design features, such as a mansard roof, low eaves, and a doorway rounded at the top to give a sense of shelter and tradition. Above all, the exterior must look well-cared for. Potential customers will draw conclusions about the food from the outside. Your exterior should be four stars.

One restaurant with no space for waiting customers built wooden benches outside the door. The lids to the benches could be lifted so that the benches could be used for storage area. The outdoor waiting area proclaimed hospitality and allowed a leisurely view of the surrounding old homes and tree-lined streets.

Chapter 9

Menus

MENUS

The restaurant menu is the guest's first substantial introduction to a restaurant, setting a vital preliminary image. The correct menu can communicate many important things to the prospective guests. For example:

"You can get a wonderful selection of food here, to fit your particular taste!"

"You can rely on my quality."

"Expect good service; we are restaurant pros and are prepared to give you good service always."

"Our prices are fair, particularly when equated with the quality of our food and fine surroundings."

Or, conversely, it can say:

"The food is so-so, and the prices are high."

The menu reflects you, your products, your reliability. Hence, it is extremely important that attention be given to its preparation. It should comprise the following elements:

1. *Attractiveness*. Does it have a pleasant first-sight impact?

2. *Readability*. Is it well-organized? Can the various types of dishes be seen quickly, at a glance? This contrasts with the menu that looks cluttered and disorganized.

3. *Distinctiveness*. How does it differ from others? How does it reflect your own restaurant personality? How does it conform with your projected "style"?

4. *Features*. Does it feature "specials"; that is, headlined meal offerings featured for any day or occasion? Most people tend to get a handle on selections when scanning a menu.

5. *Distinctiveness*. Is it distinctive in size, color, illustrations? All these factors act together to achieve the type of uniqueness that will attract guests and leave a desirable image.

Menus are designed with all types of formats and styles. "The calling card menu" of *Chuck's Steakhouse,* for example, combines a how-to-get-there map and a take-home ready reference card.

Menus can also be interlocking. This is the type of menu that folds into a square, rectangular, or pyramidical format and is commonly found in hotel rooms and coffee shops.

There's also the "VIP status symbol" type of menu. You've seen these around. These take on the appearance of impressive scrolls, tied with an ornate ribbon. This often gives the restaurant an air of exclusivity and dining elegance.

Other menu ideas include:

- *The "utilitarian" menu*. This is a dual function menu that also serves as a replaceable table mat.

- *The "mobile" menu*. This kind of menu is constantly in motion. For example, it might be chalkboard with the menu scrawled in chalk on the slateboard that is brought to the table for the patron to study.

   Some mobile menus are miniaturized: They take the form of large buttons worn by the server, announcing a current "special."

- *The "table tent" menu*. Because this kind of menu occupies a prominent position on the table and keynotes the house special—food and/or drinks—it captures priority attention.

- *The "reading matter" menu.* This type of menu may have the format of a newspaper for the guest's leisurely supplementary reading, while awaiting his meal, or any other interesting, extraneous facts that surround the food items; e.g., facts about the town, facts about the restaurant, historical data, etc.

- *The "entertainment" menu.* This contains jokes, puzzles, cartoons, etc., to absorb and regale the guest while he waits for his meal.

- *The "special events" menu.* This type of menu has the theme of a special, and usually current, event. For example, the *Small Chalet* in Chicago carried the red, white, and blue of the Bicentennial theme. It even offered ice cream in red, white, and blue, topped off with a miniature American flag.

In line with this Bicentennial theme, *Grassfield's International Restaurant* in Chicago featured a two-week American food festival. All of Dick Grossfield's restaurants ranging from New England to Hawaii, from Alaska to Florida, offered a great variety of authentically prepared American dishes.

A vast variety of American food items was served during the two-week festival. From the Southwest, sunflower seed soup, buckwheat muffins, and green beans with fatback were featured; from Hawaii, Hawaiian Moa (chicken) and Ula Tahiti (lobster with cashew). New England contributed shrimp boat salad, Cape Cod seafood combination, and Apple Brown Betty. Alaska and the Mountain States were represented by cold buckwheat pancakes and caviar and sour cream, Alaskan snowball and sourdough bread. California features included San Francisco fisherman's soup, California ranch squab, and veal cutlet Monterey. The Deep South and Florida joined the Food Festival with Cajun New Orleans' shrimp creole and bourbon sweet potatoes.

The Chicago entry was an appropriate one which demonstrated the melting pot qualities of the city: German sauerbraten with sqaetzel, Italian minnestrone soup, green pepper stuffed with Mexican corn, and Italian garlic bread were among the items featured here.

- *The "bulletin board" menu.* The changeable letters on this kind of menu simplify constant menu and price revisions.

- *The "wall" menu.* There are all types of such menus, either

Beefsteak Charlie's chalk-board design menu doubles as a table place mat.

BEEFSTEAK CHARLIE'S

"I'll feed you like there's no tomorrow."

Today's Slate

Charlie's Openers
All the Draught Beer, Wine, Sangria
or Birch Beer you can Drink with Dinner
Plus All the Salad you can make
from our Salad Bar.

Charlie's Pride & Joy

Boneless Sirloin, N.Y. Cut	5.99
Boneless N.Y. Sirloin, a Heavier Cut	6.99
Sliced Old-Fashioned Beefsteak	5.50
Filet Mignon	8.99
Barbecued Chicken	4.99
Half-Pound Steakburger on a Seeded Bun	4.99
Cheeseburger	5.29
Lobster Tails (When Available)	9.99
Sirloin Steak & Lobster Tail (When Available)	9.99
Beefsteak Charlie's Salad as a Main Course	4.99

Charlie's Side Kicks

Baked Potato, Sour Cream & Chives	.50
Sauteed Mushrooms in Butter & Sherry	1.50

Charlie's Sweet Delights

Ice Cream or Sherbet	.50
Lindy's Famous Cheesecake	1.25
Coffee, Tea or Milk	.50

Charlie's Small Fry Helpings
.99
For children under 13 accompanied by an adult ordering dinner

choice of:
2 Miniburgers on Seeded Buns
2 Hot Dogs
Barbecued Chicken

Served with Potato Chips, Soft Drink or Milk, Ice Cream or Sherbet

The Cattleman's menu is combined with chatty newspaper-type promotion with a nostalgic flavor.

MENUS

THE CATTLEMAN ENTERPRISE

Open Daily from 11:30 'til Late

GENTLEMEN IN TRADE HOLD PRIVATE POW WOWS

Cattleman Features Boots and Saddles for Business Confabs

Executives are delighted with the Cattleman's dining facilities. Business dinners are now "sound conditioned" as a result of "booths and saddles" (no saddles, really, but booths). These and other intimate areas are located throughout the emporium. Privacy is assured, but the diner never feels isolated. As one magnate put it, "You can hear one another, but no one else can." Let us hear from you as to when you'd like to reserve for such a pleasurable business dinner session.

THE PARLOURS OF MADAME MOUSTACHE

INTRIGUE RAMPANT IN UNIQUE ROOMS AT CATTLEMAN RESTAURANT

"Shocking!" exclaimed Horace Hildebund, president of the American Bluenose Society, in describing the Cattleman's Victorian "courting parlours." The "outrageous decor," as he called it, did not soften his growing resentment. The plush mohair velvet settees, the turtledoves in their gilded cages, the flickering gas lamps—tended, he felt, to create "a questionable environment." He was visibly disturbed at what he termed "promiscuous hand-holding." After being assured that Madame Moustache insisted on strict rules of proper behaviour, Mr. Hildebund was mollified, promising however that his group would continue to check on "the suspicious goings on." In making reservations, diners are advised that they may designate the room of their choice by the lady's name.

THE TRAVELLING CAESAR SALAD SHOW

The triumphant return of an old Cattleman favorite! The Caesar Salad is back and ready to be prepared at your table, compliments of Larry Ellman, Prop.

The Caesar Salad Show begins with a blend of fresh garlic and anchovies. To this, we add a squeeze of lemon, a dash of English mustard and Worcestershire sauce. A splash of vinegar and oil complete this robust dressing. To crisp Romaine, we add toasted croutons, our Caesar Dressing and the yolk of a coddled egg. A gentle toss, a sprinkle of Parmesan cheese, a turn of the pepper mill, and your Caesar Salad is complete! A perfect way to begin a most enjoyable dinner. Or, if you prefer, a large wedge of lettuce with your choice of dressing. These complimentary salads are just another special feature of the wonderful world of the Cattleman.

Six-Gun Cocktails

Restaurateurs from all parts of the country express disbelief when they hear of the Cattleman "Cocktail Credo"...offering the discerning imbiber huge-size portions at drop-in-the-bucket prices. Patrons may "name their p'izon"—Manhattans, Daiquiris, Whiskey Sours, Old Fashioneds, Rob Roys, etc.—but the most called-for concoction is that perennial rust inhibitor, the Martini-on-the-Rocks.

GREAT WESTERN GUN WORKS
Write for Large Illustrated Catalogue

A RAVE REVIEW FOR THE CATTLEMAN DIAL-A-STEAK FROM THE NEW YORK TIMES

Too mild to go out and too lazy to cook? Why not Dial-A-Steak, or lamb chops or chicken, for that matter?

Dial-A-Steak is by no means the only esteem of its kind in the city, but it's one of the better, and more efficient, of the meal delivery services. The order, whatever it may be, is at the door within an hour. If the hunger pangs are really acute, better delivery can be arranged.

The menu includes prime sirloin, double thick, for two, broiled filet mignon, lamb chops and, of course, steak. The food is quite fresh, nicely prepared. Salt, pepper, napkins and steak knives are included. (The very polite order-taker asks if you would like the knives or if you have your own. They're free, they're good, take them!)

Service is available between 4 P.M. and 11 P.M., seven days a week, and credit cards are honored. The telephone number is 593-2002.

See the article about
THE CATTLEMAN DIAL-A-STEAK on page 1, column 3.

Dr. Schilling's
HEALTH PRESERVING CORSET

Marinated Bismark Herring	1.95
Clam Casino	3.95
Oysters Rockefeller	3.95
Barbecued Baby Spareribs	3.95
French Onion Soup	1.25
Today's Soup	.95

SIDE DISHES

Toasted Garlic Bread	.75
Corn on the Cob	.50
Golden Brown Onion Rings	.75
Hot Brandied Mushrooms	1.50
Zucchini Creole	.75

PRIDE OF THE CATTLEMAN

include Caesar Salad or a Wedge of Iceberg Lettuce, potato, your choice of Sauce: Mustard, Mushroom or Oven-Fresh Bread, Creamery Butter and a Brandy or Creme de Menthe.

...eak	9.95
Top Sirloin without an ounce of fat, two inches thick, Mignon with the taste, texture and flavor of great Sirloin	
...New York Cut Sirloin Steak	10.95
...irloin, The Cattle Baron's Steak	11.95
...oned Sliced Beefsteak	8.95
...me Rib of Beef, Natural Juices	10.50
...on, Mushroom Cap	11.50
...New York Cut Sirloin Steak Sandwich	7.95
...d Beef Brochette, Buttered Rice	8.50
...Sirloin Steak, Mushroom Sauce	6.50
...ill Feast	10.95
Mixed Grill Feast for Two	14.95
Boneless New York Cut Sirloin Steak for Two	18.95
Porterhouse Steak for Two	19.95
A generous portion of the steak eater's favorite, combining the heart of the Filet Mignon with tender Sirloin. Carved from the bone, splashed with butter and served in its own juices on a hickory plank. Truly the Cattleman's Pride!	

WINE AND SANGRIA

The finest Domestic	Small	1.75
Wines, By the Carafe	Large	3.50
Sangria, By the Pitcher		3.50

DESSERTS

Rice Pudding, Whipped Cream	1.25
Ice Cream or Sherbet	1.25
Chocolate or Strawberry Sundae	1.50
Warm Apple Pie	1.25
With Cheese or Spade of Ice Cream	1.50
Cheesecake	1.75
With Strawberry Topping	
Miss Grimble's	1.75
Chocolate Orange Cheesecake or Southern Pecan Pie	
Strawberry Shortcake	1.75

BEVERAGES

Coffee, Sanka (Hot or Iced)	.75
Iced Coffee, Whipped Cream	.85
Tea (Hot or Iced)	.75
Milk	.75
Espresso	.75
Irish Bandito	1.50
Hot Coffee laced with Irish Whiskey and Kahlua, topped with fresh Whipped Cream	

Round up the Gang for group lunches, dinners, business meetings, banquets or celebrations.

Half price for Junior Outlaws (under 12) on selected entrees.

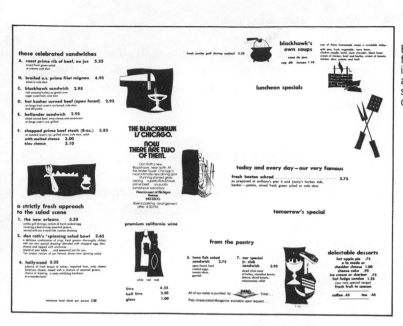

Blackhawk's menu features eye-catching illustrations...plus ample white space to separate meal categories.

those celebrated sandwiches

A. roast prime rib of beef, au jus   5.25
mixed fresh green salad or creamy cole slaw

H. broiled u.s. prime filet mignon   4.95
salad or cole slaw

C. blackhawk sandwich   2.95
rich creamed turkey au gratin over sugar cured ham, cole slaw

D. hot kosher corned beef (open faced)   2.95
on large fresh rosen's rye bread, cole slaw and dill pickle

E. hollander sandwich   2.95
sliced corned beef, swiss cheese and sauerkraut on large rosen's rye, grilled

F. chopped prime beef steak (8-oz.)   2.85
on toasted rosen's rye, grilled onion, cole slaw, relish
   with melted cheese   3.00
   bleu cheese   3.10

a strictly fresh approach to the salad scene

1. the new orleans   3.50
jumbo gulf shrimp, tomato & hard cooked egg covering a bed of crisp assorted greens, served with our irresistible russian dressing

2. don roth's *spinning salad bowl   2.65
a delicious combination of crisp, fresh greens—thoroughly chilled, with our own special dressing—blended with chopped egg, bleu cheese and topped with anchovies . . . mixed at your table . . . and seasoned just for you.
*an unique version of our famous dinner-time spinning salad.

4. hollywood   3.25
julienne of fresh breast of turkey, imported ham, swiss cheese, American cheese, tossed with a mixture of assorted greens, choice of dressing, a zesty satisfying luncheon in a wooden bowl.

minimum food check per person 2.50

THE BLACKHAWK IS CHICAGO.

NOW THERE ARE TWO OF THEM.

Don Roth's new Blackhawk, near north. At the Water Tower. Chicago's most intimate new dining spot. Stunning stained glass ceiling . . . superb Blackhawk prime beef . . . unusually sumptuous salad bar.

Pearson east of Michigan Avenue.
943-3300
liberal parking arrangement after 4:00 P.M.

premium california wine

white   red   rosé

litre   4.25
half litre   2.50
glass   1.00

blackhawk's own soups

soup du jour
cup   .60   tureen   1.10

one of these homemade soups is available today . . .
split pea, fresh vegetable, navy bean, chicken noodle, lentil, clam chowder, black bean, cream of chicken, beef and barley, cream of tomato, chicken okra, potato and leek

fresh jumbo gulf shrimp cocktail   2.25

luncheon specials

today and every day — our very famous

fresh boston schrod 3.75
as prepared at anthony's pier 4 and jimmy's harbor side,
boston – potato, mixed fresh green salad or cole slaw

tomorrow's special

from the pantry

5. tuna fish salad sandwich   2.75
open-faced, hard cooked eggs, tomato slices, garnish

7. our special jr. club sandwich   2.95
sliced white meat of turkey, canadian bacon, lettuce, sliced tomato, mayonnaise, relish

All of our water is purified by PWRO Filter . . .

Poly Unsaturated Margarine available upon request . . .

delectable desserts

hot apple pie   .75
  a la mode or
cheddar cheese   1.00
cheese cake   .95
ice cream or sherbet   .75
hot fudge sundae   1.25
(our very special recipe)
fresh fruit in season
coffee   .45   tea   .45

Don Roth's menu is easy and inviting to read.

One side of the Loop Hole's menu has a re-printed review of the restaurant. The other offers prices and a take-out number to call.

LOOP HOLE

TAKE OUTS CALL 236-6242

Soup 95
  the Day 95
O A HALF 95
y sandwich and soup   1.75

#WICHES
Beef, deli style 1.75
risket of Beef, deli style . . . 1.75
not frozen) Boston Schrod . . . 1.75
Tartar Sauce
Jumbo Frank 85

OTHER SANDWICHES
Baked Ham, deli style 1.55
Ham and Swiss 1.75
Shrimp & Egg Salad 1.45
Submarine Sandwich 1.75

Cole Slaw or Potato Salad 45

BEVERAGES
Rosé, Chablis or Burgundy Wine 65
  Mondavi of California
Schlitz Beer 50
Coca Cola, 7-Up, Root Beer, Diet Tab   .25
Milk .35
Coffee 25

DESSERTS
New York Cheese Cake 65
Special Desserts . . . . . from .55 to .55

Open 11:00 A.M. - 7:00 P.M. Daily

50 E. RANDOLPH
236-6242

THE SALAD BAR

A crisp, crunchy collection of fresh garden greens, tomatoes, mushrooms, cheeses, olives, eggs, bacon bits, etc., etc. plus homemade dressings and lots more add-ons to choose from. Always changing with the season and the whims of a perfection-prone chef.

ROAST PRIME RIBS OF BEEF

The beef that made the Blackhawk famous, aged properly and roasted to perfection. Be sure to pour on the au jus (natural juices). —NO preservatives here.
Regular or English Cut $7.95

FROM THE OPEN HEARTH BROILER

SIRLOIN STRIP — our prize winning, man's size steak — thick, juicy, tender $9.25
FILET MIGNON (9 oz.) — with fresh mushroom — everybody's favorite 7.95
PETITE FILET (6 oz.) — the same marvelous quality for the smaller appetite 6.95
CHICKEN BREAST TERIYAKI — with pineapple — polynesia at its best 5.50
CHOPPED SIRLOIN (10 oz.) — topped with sauteed mushrooms 5.50

THE BEST OF BOTH WORLDS

LOBSTER AND FILET MIGNON $9.25
BOSTON SCHROD AND FILET MIGNON 7.75
LOBSTER AND BOSTON SCHROD 8.25

BEEF OSKAR

Broiled filet mignon, crabmeat, white asparagus, and our own barnaise sauce.
Tantalizing taste treat $8.50

FISH AND SEAFOOD

FRESH BOSTON SCHROD — shipped direct from Foley's Fish Market, Boston, prepared and broiled exactly as served at Anthony's Pier 4 and Jimmy's Harbor Side, Boston $6.25

CATCH OF THE DAY — directly from the seas or lakes to your dinner plate. The freshest fish available today. Could be red snapper, whole brook or lake trout, whitefish, flounder, yellow tail, grouper, bluefish, sea bass, etc. . . . .

"COLD WATER" LOBSTER TAILS — the tender, succulent expensive kind with freshly melted butter 9.25

SEAFOOD PLATTER — french fried jumbo gulf shrimp, sea scallops, filet of boston cod, homemade tartar sauce 6.50

ALL ENTREES INCLUDE

BAKED IDAHO POTATO, with sour cream   FRESH ARTICHOKE . . . . $ .95
& chive sauce   or FRENCH FRIES   (If substituted for Potato or Spinach . . . .55)
or BLACKHAWK CREAMED SPINACH   SAUTEED FRESH MUSHROOMS 1.25

WINES AND BEVERAGES

WINE ON DRAFT — BURGUNDY, CHABLIS, ROSÉ   COFFEE, TEA, SANKA - POT .50
Liter 4.25   Half Liter 2.50   Glass 1.00   SANGRIA: Glass 1.00   Pitcher 3.95
BE SURE TO SEE OUR WINE LIST AND DESSERT MENU.

attached to the wall or built into the wall. They are made in all sizes and from all types of materials, too: from prosaic slate to rich, ornate oak and with either painted or dimensional letters.

TAKE-HOME MENUS

Some restaurants frown on their menus being taken home. Other restaurants encourage it—in fact, prepare special take-home menus for this purpose. These may be actual size or miniatures. Many experienced restaurateurs feel that the more exposure a menu has outside of the restaurant, the more valuable word-of-mouth advertising the restaurant can achieve.

CHILDREN'S MENUS

Great ingenuity is shown in the preparation of children's menus, in design, meal designation, and in diverting games. Various kinds of children's menu include:

- *The "puzzle" menu.* This is designed to keep the children quiet and absorbed for a minimum of ten minutes.
- *The "handicrafts" menu,* which is provided along with crayons. These have outlined pictures that children can color.

MENU DURATION

The frequency of menu changes varies with different restaurants, from permanent, rarely changing menus to menus that change monthly and even biweekly. No matter how frequently a menu changes, however, daily or occasional menu "specials" should be highlighted. These can be clipped or stapled to the menu, thus receiving featured attention.

Chapter 10

Children's Promotions

CHILDREN'S IMPACT ON PARENTS

Not only are children an important consideration when families decide where to eat out, but they often participate in the decisions. A 1975 study by the National Restaurant Association indicated that most parents preferred dining in family-type restaurants or coffee shops over fast food, cafeterias, or other types of restaurants. Children, on the other hand, preferred fast food places. The type of restaurants where families actually did dine out were about tied between fast foods and family-type restaurants/coffee shops. Clearly, children's preferences are decisive at least half the time.

Some other critical conclusions drawn from the study are:

- Parents took children along because children enjoyed eating out and because parents felt that dining with the whole family was an enjoyable experience.

- The most important reason parents gave for not eating out with children was that some restaurants were not geared to children.

- Parents felt that the most crucial services a restaurant could provide were children's portions and good treatment of children by personnel. A pleasurable atmosphere for children, a children's menu, the availability of special chairs, and children's beverages were also important considerations (and in that order).

Gifts were last on the parents' list. However, the fact that they were included at all shows the influence of children on their parents. Recognizing this impact, fast food chains run frequent gift promotions. In fact, many restaurants attract a substantial family trade, not only with gifts, but also with entertainment and imaginative food specialties geared to children.

Studies show that advertising dollars for ads directed toward children stretch even further than ads offered during adult prime viewing hours. Companies spend thousands of dollars and hours researching children's interests and desires. *Burger King* gave its personnel training sessions based on children's reactions. Employees were shown the spots and asked to comment, refining these ads over and over again.

Advertising directed toward children, making the point that children have individual tastes, is an effective beginning to promoting family trade. Burger King, for example, ran television ads on the chain's "Have it your way" theme, using children in adult masks trying to eat hamburgers. When they don't succeed, the children take off their masks, showing that their taste in food is different from adults', and that Burger King considers the personal taste of even children. The children in this ad are given names like Picklish, Nickelish, and Peter Piper.

FOOD PROMOTION SPECIALTIES FOR CHILDREN

A family Sunday brunch geared toward togetherness is a basic promotion requiring no extras, except a lower price for children's portions. A card with a drawing of a family can be put on tables during the week, so that it can be easily seen by diners who may remember it when considering where to take the children on Sunday.

Special bargains on children's meals will attract parents. Offer a free beverage. When adults order a full meal, children's meals are half-price. There are several variations on this for families. The first child under a certain age eats free, the second child under the age limit eats at a large discount, and all other children's meals are at the standard price.

To attract family business, Holiday Inn set aside a three-month period when children would receive all three meals free. Items had to be chosen from a specific menu. A crunchy cereal, bacon and eggs, or bacon and pancakes were on the breakfast menu, while lunch and dinner selections included peanut butter and jelly, chicken or hamburger and French fries, Beefaron, a hot dog, and potato chips. You might want to adapt such a promotion for slow periods in your restaurant.

Present food imaginatively. *Dunkin' Donuts* has turned doughnuts into a separate product line with a new name, "Dunkin' Munchkins." The variety of Munchkins is similar to doughnuts: chocolate, honey-glazed, jelly-filled.

If you serve exotic food, don't automatically write yourself off the children's market. Advertise children's portions, and a magician, clown, or perhaps a character dressed in clothes from the country that your menu features.

CHILDREN'S MENUS AND PLACE MATS

Children's menus can be a child-pleasing strategy in and of themselves. They can be specially designed in a toy-oriented format, such as the shape of a railroad train, a circus wagon, or an animal. The menu can double as a game book, with connect-the-dot drawings or alphabet games, match each letter of the alphabet with some symbol, write a sentence using the symbols, and then ask the children to translate the symbols so they form a sentence.

The same can be done with place mats, either in addition to, or instead of, menus. You can also give a miniature crayon box with a few crayons to each child.

ENTERTAINMENT

Playgrounds

A playground can be scaled up or down, according to your budget. This, of course, requires outdoor space. Start with a few

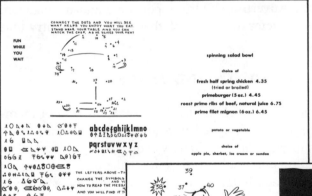

This book jacket from the International House of Pancakes offers a real treat for kids that they will carry out of the restaurant and show to others.

This menu contains fun for kids.

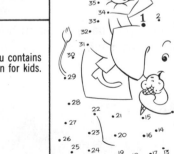

FOLLOW THE DOTS AND COLOR WITH CRAYON

IN NEW YORK...
RESTAURANTS · NIGHT CLUBS · HOTELS

Both the Cattleman and Steer Palace feature children's specials.

The Holiday Inn advertises for summer travelers.

Nathan's Famous features weekly kiddie shows.

This menu attracts children's birthday parties.

swings, a monkey bar, and a seesaw. Add sculpural forms a child can climb through. Playgrounds can cost a minimum amount by recycling old materials such as automobile tires as swings. The ground should be covered in a soft, flexible material, since there are bound to be falls. In fact, *Gino's* in Philadelphia has built several playgrounds as a community service.

Children's Theater

Children's theater boils down to puppet shows and magicians. Hire a professional entertainer to give performances on Sunday afternoon, a big dining-out day for families. Perhaps there's a roving troupe in your area that sets up a theater in a truck, and that can perform a short play with scenery, costumes, and colorful characters. These plays, often updated fairy tales, can often make up in energy what they lack in expensive decoration. Like the playground, however, such a venture requires some additional space. However, this can be arranged by folding up chairs and tables and using the dining room as a theater.

Magicians, ventriloquists, and clowns going from table to table entertain children without taking them from the family gathering. Balloons, blown up before the children's eyes and taking on weird shapes, are another portable entertainment. At the *Cattleman* a former vaudeville team dresses as Mrs. Clown and Mr. Sheriff and goes from table to table inflating balloons and performing a few magic tricks.

A guest appearance by a television personality well-known to children will bring families in droves. But the guest must show up and be there when the children are. When a commitment to children falls through, there are angry parents to deal with as well as restless kids.

For two months *Nathan's,* famous in New York City, made up flyers listing its Sunday kiddie shows (at 1 and 3 P.M.). The shows, which were free, included a puppet performance of Mozart's opera, "The Magic Flute," a "minimusical comedy" song, dance and audience participation, fairy tale productions, and several magicians.

Cartoons

Another possibility, if you have the space, is to turn a room into a movie house and show cartoons on Sunday afternoons. *The Cattleman,* a New York City steakhouse, includes a three-hour program of cartoons among its various entertainment programs for children. The restaurant has a stagecoach and driver in cowboy clothes which it uses for promotional purposes—among them, giving children a ten-minute ride in the coach.

Storytelling

Or, set aside a separate area for storytelling. All this requires is a reader sympathetic to children, a good children's book, and a clean floor for children to sit on.

Use of Animals

Create an animal symbol for children to play on or to entertain the children. This can be used to emphasize your children's products and promotions at sales meetings, on television, and in the restaurant. The Friendly Ice Cream Corporation invented "Scoopy the Bear," and someone dressed in fuzzy paws and a large teddy bear head mask dances for the children. "Scoopy" is accompanied by a waitress who hands out puppets and balloons and answers questions about the company. The dancing bear was originally used as an internal training ad. Gradually, it appeared in coloring books, on balloons, and finally in media campaigns.

BIRTHDAY PROMOTIONS

Keep a book where children's birthdays can be recorded when families come in for the first time. Notify the child that when his birthday is coming up, a free birthday cake will be available for him if he celebrates at your restaurant. On premise, mark a special holiday with a treat, such as a spook giving out cookies on Hallowe'en.

Make birthday parties a featured attraction, even if you are essentially a fast food restaurant. Nathan's makes an exception to its self-service policy for birthday parties by providing waiters. Besides a choice of birthday cakes with candles, the menu includes a frankfurter or hamburger, French fries, and a choice of drinks. Nathan's also supplies birthday decorations: tablecloths, napkins, party hats, and favors for a minimum party of ten. The cost is about $3.00 a person.

To promote off-premises or take-home promotions, the brochure that promotes children's birthday parties also points out that the chain has a buffet catering service for the home or office, and a special consultant to help plan off-premises events.

GIVE-AWAYS OR DISCOUNT PROMOTIONS

One chain of restaurants publicized a 99 cent "children's travel kit" to amuse children when they are traveling in a car or playing at home. The kit included bingo games, the restaurant ad and insignia, a cowboy gun, a cardboard Indian hat, and a sketch book. This kind of promotion guarantees that the name of your restaurant will be remembered long after the family has visited.

GENERAL PROMOTIONS FOR CHILDREN

Other possible promotion ideas for children are:
- Perform a public service while you promote your restaurant. Invite school children to tour your restaurant. Explain how pastry is made, salad is prepared, or where different cuts of meat come from. A large commercial kitchen is a mystery for children, since they see things they don't usually see at home when their mother or father is cooking.
- Set up a scholarship. It need not be large; $50 to cover the expense of books and other school supplies. The fund should be given every semester or every year, a recurring reminder that you care about your community.
- On the less serious side, sponsor a dance contest for teen-agers. Set aside part of your restaurant for this, or rent a local hall. Work with other food and drink provisioners.
- Sponsor wall paintings by children. The wall can be a fence around a play enclosure or a blank, ugly wall in your town that would be enlivened by a little paint. You supply the brushes and paint.
- Put a treasure chest or grab bag near the door. Children can reach in and pull out a surprise—an inexpensive toy at no charge.
- Balloons inscribed with the name of your restaurant can be a memorable good-bye gift for children.

- Hand out buttons with mottos that tie in with your restaurant:"Steak power."
- Puppets with your name on them for children to take them home are lasting reminders of your restaurant.
- Book covers or book marks are a versatile publicity tool. They are useful, they indirectly reinforce the idea of education, and they can be designed for entertainment, with jokes, puzzles, pictures, and also your name (although this should not dominate the cover) on them.
- The most entertaining gifts should be connected with a large purchase. A family buying a bucket of chicken for $5 (or $10) or more might either receive a toy airplane free, or might choose from among several gifts.
- Offer a free Hallowe'en "trick or treat" kit with a big box of doughnuts or some other take-out item in your restaurant. The kit should contain a mask and reflecting armband to wear at night, and can come in a bag that can be used to carry candies and pennies on Hallowe'en night.

Before deciding on a promotion item, study catalogues of the companies that manufacture them before deciding on which model or item to use. This will give you a good idea of the price and item range of gifts.

One word of warning, however: A promotion item can have just the opposite effect you intend if it annoys parents. Avoid any promotion that has a piercing whistle; it will destroy a parent's peace of mind and can result in negative associations with the restaurant.

Chapter 11

Group Sales

If you've ever spent a grim evening watching a heavy rain instead of customers, you've probably considered soliciting tour groups or working out a series of eye-catching special promotions. But when the rain stops and the regulars are back the next night, somehow there's never quite enough time to plan for the future.

Consider how you would have welcomed a group of ten or twenty people on that rainy night. Think of having had a group of people who would have braved the rain for "a different kind of dining experience." And then think of the overhead—the waiters, gas, electricity, food and rent—you had to pay for nothing that night.

ATTRACTING NEW BUSINESS

Increasing your pool of potential customers begins with a very clear idea of the character of your restaurant: Is it intimate and unpretentious? Is it sleek and modern? Is it for families? Do people come to socialize or do business, or both? In asking these questions, also consider if there's anything you'd want to change or if there's a potential clientele you're not getting. Appealing for customers beyond the present range of your store also helps to increase both your patronage and your profitability.

Special promotions not only attract, but also help to maintain, new business. Don't wait until business is bad. Work out your ideas and experiment with them when the pressure is especially low.

Special promotions touch people's interests, tastes, sense of humor, and pocketbooks. They mean that you're giving your customers a bargain. The majority of your special promotions should emphasize food. Too many promotions emphasizing other aspects of the restaurant will look like you're apologizing for the menu, not pointing to it with pride. Be careful not to overpromote your operation.

Local changes and events can not only confirm that your image is right for your market, but can also make you decide to update it. Suppose a housing development goes up nearby, and you want the young, well-paid residents at your restaurant. You might decide upon a new paint job, checkered table cloths, flowers, and candlelight on the table. You might also take ham and processed cheese off the menu while adding a curry dish. After all this, it's time for the promotions. Don't expect that everything will happen all at once. It will take more than one promotion to build up a steady new clientele.

TOURS

Tours can be either a disaster or a life-saver. They are particularly worth considering if you have a lot of space to fill. Space, however, isn't the sole consideration. Image is also an important consideration. The identity you have carefully established is one of the factors that your regular patrons enjoy. A large group of strangers may simply not belong in your restaurant. Talk to travel agents. Find out what kind of crowd a particular convention or meeting brings in and judge whether they'll find your restaurant in line with their expectations. Perhaps there are a few unusually small tour or sports groups coming to or passing through your area. See if any would fit into your restaurant. If so, perhaps you can make some arrangements. But find out how many people are involved.

A busful of 55 people, for example, might overwhelm your

dining room. Perhaps they could be divided among several neighboring restaurants. Your best clues as to the kind of groups you'll get are the local attractions that bring the groups. Craft or produce fairs, scenic stretches of beach, a restored historic town, an important golf tournament in the state: Each will bring in a different clientele with different tastes and different needs.

In attracting large groups of people you'll probably have to work with other businesses in the area. A nearby hotel or motel with no eating facilities might be interested in having catered meals, especially breakfast. A continental breakfast—sweet rolls and coffee—is simple to prepare and deliver, although you may also want to add juice, cereal, or eggs to the menu. List the choices on a card to be left in each room. Guests can check off what they want, note the time it is desired, and hang the card on the outside doorknob. The desk clerk can call in the orders in the early morning and at other times during the day.

TAKE-OUT MEALS

Selling travelers on a relaxing meal while they're on their way somewhere else might be difficult. Still, hunger must be satisfied somewhere. Prepare a stylishly boxed take-out meal. It should be: 1) able to be eaten on a lap, 2) food that doesn't spoil easily, 3) tasty, even hours after it has been prepared, and 4) wrapped in advance with plastic utensils, napkins, salt, and pepper, so that only beverages have to be prepared individually.

Make your picnic meal the superstar of take-out foods in your area. Advertise the pleasure of biting into your fresh potato salad. Size up the picnic potential of local attractions and direct your advertising toward their visitors. Are you near a beach, a state park, scenic mountains, a hunting preserve, a marina, a theater with a large landscaped area around it, a crafts or produce fair? If so, make the most of them.

Those versatile picnic meals can tour such local sights. If a tour traditionally stops at a restaurant other than yours, perhaps you can convince them to take a box lunch to a particularly lovely spot in the country where tourists can eat al fresco. Discuss this possibility with the tour director.

BUSINESS AND ENTERTAINMENT POSSIBILITIES

Theaters or festivals some distance from a city may have buses exclusively serving that area. Why not plan a special pretheater supper? Or, after arranging a package with the theater, offer ticketholders a ten percent discount and advertise it in and around the city.

If you are in a part of the country known for a particular kind of food, highlight the uniqueness of your area by offering a special price for regional dishes. When conventions are in town, a New England restaurant, for example, prices a lobster dinner low if it is ordered before 6 P.M. It also sends out mailings to these large groups a month before the convention is held.

Try to develop cooperative recreation packages for business conventions. After being in a conference all day, many business people want some exercise. Tie your program in with sports facilities. Make your restaurant a center for sports information. A gym or health club, riding academy, golf course, or tennis club might lower their rates at certain times—say, early morning—while you give a 10% discount between the hours of 5 and 7. Once the package is set up, it can be repeated for political and social organizations, card clubs, tours for families or single people, class reunions, and other groups.

If your town isn't a lodestone for tourists, you can help to put it on the road to being one. Start with local tourist agencies to find out what immediate attractions there are in your town, and what more distant attractions might draw outsiders across your path. Travel publications, as well as the general and travel sections in magazines and newspapers, are loaded with both travel attractions and names of organizations to contact for more information. Try to contact the people who direct these attractions and see if you can arrange some mutually beneficial agreements with them. If not, perhaps you can persuade them to let you leave brochures at least.

Once you have exhausted these possibilities, contact travel agencies. Invite the director for a free meal next time he or she is passing through town and suggest your restaurant as a place where tourists can combine excellent dining with relaxation during their hectic schedules. Don't overlook the importance of time; mention that you're prepared to serve, say, 35 people at one time in an hour at a leisurely pace so that everyone can enjoy the meal. Send a menu and point out your specialties, emphasizing the dishes that would be easiest to prepare for large groups. While the tour director might want to leave the ordering to each individual sightseer, he or she might still be able to predict their choices with some degree of accuracy so that you'll be able to prepare in advance.

Also check out commercial bus companies. If it will help business, point out the need for a stop near your restaurant. Even if the bus stays only long enough to pick up or discharge passengers, waiting travelers are business for you.

To accommodate nationwide bus tours, *Howard Johnson's* has a toll-free "800" number so that reservations for large groups can be made in advance. Howard Johnson's also gives the locations of the chain's restaurants along the various bus routes. In fact, meal cards and information were sent to 1,500 bus and tour companies across the country, offering free meals to the bus drivers and tour directors who brought in business.

Other entertainment possibilities include: music festivals, summer stock theaters, horse shows, dog shows, stock car races, horse races, fashion shows, football, rodeos, dance festivals, historic areas.

Military bases also get a lot of visitors. While you can't advertise in the base itself, check out local newspapers or off-base places that attract a lot of military personnel.

STAGED EVENTS

Staged and special events can be an enormous drawing card. A Las Vegas hotel, for example, held a gourmet cooking demonstration by the executive chef of Weight Watchers. The demonstration had five co-sponsors, including a home economics college, an appliance store, a utility company, Weight Watchers, and the hotel. A three-quarter page newspaper ad showed the smiling chef and listed free prizes that would be distributed.

You can even plan and stage your own "group demonstration" events. This can include unusual ethnic foods, low-calorie meals, preparation of gourmet meals, new cooking techniques, meals that men can cook, and so on. There are endless ideas, each of which can attract literally crowds of local people seeking this kind of knowledge. What's more, along with business, you'll also achieve splendid public relations exposure.

This idea can be scaled down to lesser proportions, of course.

If you need new ideas, there's no end to the cookbooks published every season for every possible kind of person. In fact, cookbooks can be the source of demonstrators for your event. After all, think of all the cookbooks that have appeared in the last few years. There are books for people who hate cooking and who love it, books for people who want to cook only intimate dinners for two and for people who must cope with as many as ten. There are books for dieters, health-food addicts, and every conceivable ethnic group.

The popularity of such books attests to the interest that cooking holds for people. Their authors, in fact, often make cross-country publicity tours. Why not contact the publishing companies that put these books out to arrange for a demonstration at your restaurant? Local cooking schools might even let you use their mailing list. Talk to your customers. You'll pick up ideas about the kind of cooking that interests them.

A few years ago, Chinese cooking threatened to supersede French cuisine as number one among home chefs. Many people and restaurants gave woks for Christmas. Chinese cooking achieved this popularity because of people's new interest in and craving for vegetables, because of the rising price of meat, and because of the increasing emphasis on good diet.

PUBLICIZE TRENDS

When you recognize a trend like this, call the local newspaper and talk to the editor of homemaking features. Or, if you discover that an author of one of these books lives in your neighborhood, arrange a demonstration. The demonstration can have a practical angle: It can pinpoint or attract a particular market—say, the single homemaker. "Five great dishes that can be made in a kitchenette," or, "The gourmet guide for single people" (or "single parents": Contact a local single parents organization for your audience). The local round of renowned chefs can be found in private clubs, corporations, and restaurants, and aren't considered competitors.

Scan your clientele for prestigious citizens who like to cook and their favorite dishes: the mayor's celebrated bean salad, for example, or a famous athlete's chicken Kiev. Feature a particular specialty for a week, inviting its creator for dinner. Be sure to be on hand the first night that his or her pièce de résistance is served. You might decide to incorporate Charlie Dodson's lobster newburg permanently on the menu.

As a one-time event, however, several local gourmet cooks can demonstrate their greatest dishes in different parts of your restaurant. Serve a buffet supper that night. This will encourage people to wander around and watch. This can be a particularly effective promotion for a charitable cause.

HOST A RADIO SHOW

A radio talk show that emanates from your restaurant is automatic advertising. Discuss this possibility with the director of your local radio station and a columnist or highly articulate personality to host the show on a weekly basis. The host will invite well-known people who will add to the prestige of your restaurant. Or, have your chef give out new cooking ideas and recipe suggestions. Refreshments for the participants are, of course, on the house.

Are you located in a center for aspiring actors, actresses, and comedians? They will often work for free to get exposure and experience before an audience. Once a month hold a Stardust Night. The month gives you or an employee time to audition acts. This event could be held on a slow night, possibly coming at a night when the night theaters are closed, so that working performers can also participate. In reverse, you can feature a particularly promising performer on weekends.

Generally speaking, it's best to restrict entertainment to areas where only drinks are consumed, to avoid distracting performers and patrons alike. Fully professional live entertainment is expensive, requiring a volume of $400 to $500 a day to support a good attraction. It should therefore be scheduled during your greatest volume of business. Be sure that live entertainment is right for you. If it is, get the best you can afford. And let everyone know about it.

DINNER THEATER

Carry the dinner plus entertainment concept to its fullest conclusion and you have a dinner theater. While generally thought of as dinner in a theater rather than theater in a restaurant, a dinner theater is likely to be a large scale enterprise with a stage equipped for completely professional productions. The Midnight Sun Dinner Theater in Atlanta is a cooperative venture by a restaurant company, a company specializing in dinner theaters, and Actors' Equity. The 525 seat, $2.5 million entertainment and dining package was developed by one of the nation's most creative architects in hotel and commercial centers. Dinner features a smorgasbord that includes roast prime ribs. Tickets are priced from $15.00 to $18.00. Matinees and children's productions were planned to begin after the dinner theater had opened.

A dinner theater package can be created through a joint promotion by a theater and restaurant located near each other. They jointly offer parking at a minimal rate. Promotional literature should give the telephone number of your restaurant for reservations, since people generally make theater arrangements first and often don't consider dinner until the last minute.

Dinner theater promotions can be expanded and varied to fit different groups. A "weekend for two" directed to parents who want a vacation alone without children and household responsibilities would include a hotel, possibly museum tours or athletic events, and a second evening's entertainment. A restaurateur who owns several establishments, particularly if the restaurants differ in mood and menu, can be the most important element in the package.

Running the same event periodically gives repeated opportunity for promotion. Art shows are truly distinctive events, good image makers (whether you have an abstract painting or a portrait, you're an art lover), and attractions bound to draw some customers that are art patrons. You will have to look into the cost of insurance and setting up the exhibit to know if an art show falls within your budget. Don't forget, however, that it draws a very desirable, and often wealthy, clientele.

Such an event encourages the mingling of diverse groups. This kind of crowd can add to your reputation as a knowledgeable person who knows everyone worth knowing in town. The artist can drop by and become the center for a group who comes to socialize with him.

LIVE MUSIC

Put some contemporary gaiety into an historic occasion with live entertainment. Inquire around a college campus for a good singing group. Dressed in jeans, workshirts, and red bandannas, entertainers can wander around the room minstrel style, can perform as singing waiters, or can perform onstage at a specific time. One note of caution: When people come primarily to eat, the more casual the entertainment, the better. Definitely avoid amplified guitars. They drown out all conversation and send customers away for good.

The repertoire can include songs on the theme of the holiday, interspersed with pop music. Encourage customer requests; it gives the diners a sense of participation and individual attention. If you feel that a minstrel group is not formal enough for your place, there's no reason you can't have a violinist instead.

Pianos have always been a great favorite for diners. A good piano player adds instant sophistication and atmosphere to any eatery. It is live music that requires little space. And while a regular performing musician might be too expensive to keep on a payroll, the occasional (special holidays only) accompanist may be more in line with what you can afford. Even if you go somewhat over budget, it may be worth your while in the long run. After all, it conveys the sense of being in an intimate and specific place; not just any of ten restaurants serving steaks and roast beef in modern decor, but your own very specific place. If the piano is a roaring success on special occasions, you might use it on a more regular basis; say, Friday and Saturday nights.

Most of your customers probably prefer a piano as a pleasant background to conversation. But at some time or other everyone likes to get up close. Dramatize the music without letting it dominate the room by encircling the piano with a bar, or by having a bar close to the musicians. Your biggest problem will be getting people away to give others a chance.

Remember, too, that the most winning music does not necessarily come from a professional musician. Many amateurs that go unnoticed can be a goldmine. Beneath many a pinstripe suit is a snappy piano player who once performed professionally but will now play for the pleasure of having an audience. Many others would like extra money for college or for their kids' education. Local and business people with an arty side have been cropping up in many suburban areas. Take a hard look at yours.

Once you've taken the leap to live music, it's only a short walk to dancing. You certainly don't have to give half your restaurant over to a dance floor, nor must it be permanent. On special occasions, however, you can roll out a heavy plastic mat, push aside a few tables, and let your customers enjoy the music by dancing between courses. Consider it a floor show that doesn't interfere with conversation or serving dinner, and you'll be amazed at the number of dancers who can fit into an incredibly small space. This can be terrific for Valentine's Day, and there's no reason why dancing won't work on July 4th or Thanksgiving as well.

HOLIDAY PROMOTIONS

Americans are a spartan lot when it comes to national holidays. They don't celebrate with week-long carnivals or dancing in the streets, as Europeans do. Instead, they celebrate by eating and being with their families. During holiday seasons, you can serve a simple turkey dinner for just about any occasion.

About a week before the holiday—Thanksgiving, Christmas, Labor Day—run an ad that shows the menu. Be sure to note that large parties are welcomed with advance reservations.

To keep holidays wrapped in their tradition, serve one or more specialties taken from old recipes used by townsfolk years ago. A local historical society should be able to help you find the recipes. The original recipes can be reproduced on cards (use the antique spelling) and given to customers.

Be sure to use these authentic dishes in your advertising. In your ads or on your menus give them a name—"Mrs. Wordsworth's lickered ham"—and include a folksy biography of Mrs. Wordsworth that will tell people something about the people and their town one hundred years ago.

On Washington's Birthday, two different restaurants offered promotions that projected two entirely different images. One midwestern restaurant offered a free slice of cherry pie with dinner. Patrons considered this a bargain. While it lacked panache, it nevertheless conveyed a solid, stable, conservative image. This worked fine in the midwestern community, where families liked the idea of a bargain, and where style was a minor consideration.

But if you are drawing your clientele from an urban area, free pie will probably not be a "knock-'em-dead" promotion. Many urbanites are free with their money and expect to spend it in return for being catered to through food and ambiance. When they come to your place, they expect you to consider them discriminating gourmets who know how to live well. For these people, free cherry pie won't provide much excitement for your image or much inducement for potential diners.

Sage's East runs constant promotions. Naming February "Liar's Month," the restaurant gave its customers a folder with a picture of George Washington. Inside, customers were asked to write a good old-fashioned lie, and were given some examples: "It's not the money . . . it's the principle." "To be perfectly honest with you. . . ." "I'm not prejudiced, but. . . ." "My wife doesn't understand me." "He hit me first." Prizes for the cleverest "lies" were given out on Washington's Birthday, February 22nd. This promotion was a hit, because the urban Chicago diners enjoyed the feeling of being convivial, witting souls, and they welcomed the opportunity to display their imagination and creativity.

Two different *Sage* establishments made use of St. Patrick's Day to draw business. Recognizing that many of their patrons who worked hard also played hard, one establishment proclaimed a three-day St. Patrick's Day bash, featuring a variety of "fun events" involving customer participation. These included telling one's best jokes or best stories (also the worst jokes and the worst stories), performing humorous skits, parodies, etc. The event was intended to reinforce the very distinct impression that Sage customers are fast-talking, hard-drinking, witty guys with a sharp but discriminating appetite.

Another St. Patrick's Day promotion promised "something" for any written limerick that was presented to the restaurant on St. Patrick's Day. Along with this, the eatery offered Irish pennies, four-leaf clovers, Irish Mist, misty-eyed Irish songs, Irish fun, and corned beef and cabbage.

You need not necessarily be bound by conventional holidays, however. There's always something worth celebrating. And if an occasion escapes you for the moment, make one up. *Eugene's* held a belated first anniversary party. Champagne and hors d'oeuvres were served for an anniversary party that was held two months after the anniversary date. A good time for a no-occasion event is in mid-January, when the post-New Year's blahs have set in. The bait could be excellent wine at a reasonable price, or even a wine and cheese tasting event (always a hit).

Whether it's a president or a referendum, Americans have something to vote for at least once a year. Celebrate the election with a cocktail event or a buffet dinner a few weeks before the election. (You will want people to move around and talk to each other.) Your ad could begin, "We run the best political parties," followed with the announcement of the event: "Everyone is invited to come and argue their point of view. And if the opposition doesn't get to you, our well-equipped bar will." As an added attraction, free or discount drinks could be served to anyone in the bar at a specific time. You could ring a bell at 5:36, for instance, and everyone who is there at that time can get a round on the house.

FAMILY DINNERS FOR SOLOS

Celebration might be a tradition in many families, but in many homes people are alone and left to feel like social pariahs in the midst of all togetherness season. The divorced, the single, the businessperson in a strange town, the elderly: All can suffer from loneliness. To help them, why not set aside a large table (unless you're sure it will work, set it for no more than six), and as you seat single customers, ask them if they would like to sit at your family-style table, rather than at a private table. Always give the customer the choice. You might even want to give a special half-price discount to senior citizens.

SPECIAL EVENTS

Another promotion idea that can be loads of fun is a ridiculous beauty pageant. Hold a contest for the most beautiful ear, nose, big toe, or wrist. And give fitting prizes to the winner: ear or nose plugs, nail polish, tennis or golf wristbands.

Sage's East bought a block of tickets for the opening of a film that was sure to be sold out. Customers could reserve tickets, which the restaurant distributed on the night of the performance. The restaurant saved diners the trouble of standing in line or going out of their way for the tickets; the diners paid the boxoffice price without having to do anything more than eat at the restaurant.

Don Roth's Blackhawk restaurant in Chicago runs fashion as well as art shows. As many as two lunch hour shows a week are held, each in conjunction with another well-known department store.

INTERNATIONAL EVENTS

Special events can be exotic as well as historic. On the exotic side there are travel themes. Proclaim a Night in Rio (Alcapulco, Paris, Biarritz, Casablanca). Carry out the theme with multimedia effects—lighting, music, and scenic views projected on a wall or the ceiling. Roll out the dance floor and hire entertainment for the night.

Create a gourmet inner sanctum for diners interested in banqueting on superb authentic French cuisine. Establish a gourmet society. Invite interested patrons to a round of four to six dinners a year (but hold many more than that yourself, limiting the number of diners at any one event to about twenty-five. This will help maintain a sociable, privileged atmosphere that can be enhanced with an array of outstanding wines and haute cuisine). Members of Sage's East Société au Gourmet Extraordinaire paid $25.00 for a picnic in the French countryside or at a chateau (the dinners had different themes), including tips and taxes.

Simulating an international festival or foreign custom is also fun. A German Oktoberfest or beer hall; the French Bastille Day or outdoor cafe; Denmark's Tivoli Gardens: All are possibilities for special events. In fact, these international themes are particularly adaptable to wine-tasting events accompanied by cheeses of the appropriate nation.

AMERICA'S PAST

America has produced enough great composers, musicians, film stars, artists, and historical figures to inspire hundreds of nostalgia trips. You can celebrate a decade—the 1920's, 1930's, or 1940's. Talk to a music buff and pin down a particularly rich year in jazz or show music. Hire live musicians. Rent clips from well-known films of the period and use them as background. You might want to install a few temporary decorative motifs like palm trees that were popular in the 1950's.

Artwork and paintings can be rented from museums and private dealers for the evening. A special menu can be devised with a design in keeping with the period and featuring dishes invented for the occasion: sliced steak à la Rogers and Astaire, or a Western omelette à la John Wayne. If political buttons from the period can be found, use them as a decorative motif in the restaurant. You might even want to draw them as bubbles rising from a champagne glass in advertising the event.

Research into local history will probably produce many incidents, both serious and funny, that can be promoted into a special event worth toasting at your bar. Do some research on important battles, heroes, and heroines. The better storytellers at your watering-hole will recall amusing events that are less than history but have the makings of a legend.

You can even make a special event out of looking for an event. Get out the fancy hors d'oeuvres for a cocktail hour devoted to a contest for good local tales. Hand out cards on which the stories, names, and addresses can be written, with a prize for the best idea. You can even invent a drink and name it for a local folk hero. Why not "Muldoon's milk (vodka, rum, vermouth)"?

Another simple and effective way of creating a specific image for your restaurant is to identify it with a well-known and well-liked literary character or public personality. This can be extremely valuable in differentiating several restaurants under the same ownership. *Eugene's,* for example, is identified with Damon Runyon, whose tales of hearts-of-gold dames and gambling gents in New York City are American classics. And if anyone missed the classic stories, they've probably seen the classic American musical, *Guys and Dolls.* Sage customers are constantly reminded of this in any publicity connected with Eugene's:

"So EUGENE'S has tried to measure up to the fun, the excitement, the class and the eclectic food tastes of the Runyon characters. They may have been temporarily down and out, but even at their lowest ebb they would not tolerate inferior food—even in a simple cup of java. Neither will we," reads early promotional literature, clearly stating the connection between the restaurant and Runyon.

TIE-IN WITH OTHER BUSINESSES AND RESTAURANTS

Any locality with any pretensions to a tropical climate abounds in swimming pools. Many of them are not used frequently or are not used at certain times during the day. Perhaps you can rent the pool for an affair. This could be a lunch or dinner for a guest of honor with a special barbecue, a fashion show—both men's and women's—or the opening of an important new company This kind of promotion will probably have to be done cooperatively with you as the caterer. You will need a source of clothes, flowers, tables, chairs, and music. Together with other sponsors you could arrange a diving or swimming competition for children or adults, using the pool for more than a lovely setting.

Mergers and other changes in your corporate status are public relations opportunities. Take advantage of their publicity potential. *Orsi's* in Chicago wrote to its customers and announced a merger with an automotive service company. The locations of the auto service centers, as well as special services they offered, were also mentioned. Coupons for both a free car wash at the service center and a free drink at Orsi's were enclosed with the letter.

A variation of this is to tie-in with a bank (or banks) in your area. Offer "free meals for two" to new bank customers. The bank pays for the meals, usually at an agreed-upon discount. Many banks find this to be a good promotional approach in generating new accounts, and restaurants get added publicity exposure (since the banks publicize them in their ads) and also profit from the resulting patronage.

If you're in a densely populated urban center, you're probably surrounded by restaurants quite different from your own. So why not suggest a cooperative effort with the two nearest you? On the same night, arrange to have all three restaurants serve an "all-you-can-eat," buffet style smorgasbord of each restaurant's specialties. Tickets bought at any one restaurant should be good at all three. Diners can move among the three restaurants, sampling various dishes they might never have considered ordering. Having sampled tastes of various exotic dishes, however, you can bet that they'll come back again.

Alcohol need not be included in the price of the meal. Receipts could be divided according to a total count of all the people who have eaten in each restaurant, according to the percentage of food consumed, or equally, regardless of other factors. This should be decided in advance.

You might already have applied the smorgasbord concept to your own cocktail hour hors d'oeuvres, serving small bits of fried chicken, meatballs, spare ribs, and cold foods between 5 and 7 P.M.

To go sparingly on the hot hors d'oeuvres or on something like a steak tartare, which is too expensive to be anything other than a prestige item, serve these foods at a specific time. A waiter can go around with an hors d'oeuvres tray halfway through cocktail time, rather than leaving them out for the whole period.

Several other promotion ideas that tend to encourage group sales are listed below.

● Install a ticker tape. This encourages the business crowd and makes it very clear that your restaurant caters to busy executives. One New York restaurant put one in the center of its entranceway.

● Keep a television on hand for important sports events. It can be a big draw on Saturday afternoons, when business is slow.

● Set aside a small room off the bar as a game area, with a pool table, and pinball machines, including electronic tennis games and other new variations.

● Chess and backgammon tables can be included either in a game room or in another, separate area to draw lunchtime crowds. In fact, the table can be designed as a shallow box, divided in half, with the bottom part a permanent game board. With the lid on, however, this gameboard can become a table for dining and cock-tails. If people come to use the game boards, charge a minimum of one dollar an hour for gameplayers.

● Antique chairs are promotable, permanent decor. Rummage through used furniture stores to find chairs of interesting shapes and with good carving. Scrape the old paint off, stain the wood, and you have an antique. The chairs should not match; their variety gives a dramatic quality to your restaurant. Mention your antique furnishings in your advertising.

● The natural environment around your restaurant is part of the decor. Don't hide a view of the ocean. Advertise it: "Have a sun-set on the rocks. . . ."

● Put out a monthly or weekly bulletin listing all the events for the coming days, with a brief, light-hearted description. These handouts should be well-designed and printed on colored paper.

Chapter 12

Banquet Sales Promotions

Banquets can be very profitable for restaurants. They help to achieve the following:

- They attract volume patronage from many organizations and many types of events.
- They attract new customers to your place who would not ordinarily patronize your restaurant. Based on their satisfaction with the food and surroundings, they often come back on their own, also recommend friends.
- They provide a welcome flow of "prescheduled" business, so the restaurateur can plan amply in advance both personnel-wise and space-wise.

WHO ARE BANQUET PROSPECTS?

Banquet prospects include a wide range of potential groups that include:

1. Companies (of various types) commemorating a variety of events such as:

   - Sales meetings
   - Celebration of specific accomplishments
   - Commemoration of a particular employee or employer
   - Business conferences
   - Regional and nationwide conclaves
   - Various types of meetings, conventions, etc.

2. The General Public. These banquet events include:

   - Family meetings
   - Special events—weddings, barmitzvas, engagements, etc.
   - Clubs, associations, tour groups, etc.

This type of business offers a veritable gold mine of opportunity to the restaurant, often enabling long-term, 100% patronage. This type of business is constantly available; it just requires asking. The restaurateur should make regular contacts of eligible companies and organizations, and should also contact conventions scheduled to visit the city.

Start your banquet sales campaign as soon as you have signed a lease for a site. To achieve maximum results in the shortest possible time, your banquet program should be well-organized and developed promptly.

Procedures for a successful banquet sales campaign include:

1. Determine all the markets for banquet sales, and develop mailing lists and solicitation lists. Your market should include major business firms, fraternal organizations, charitable organizations, sales organizations, churches, religious clubs, etc.

2. Send a mailing, tailored to each of these specific groups. Examples of mailings are contained on the following pages.

3. Follow up these mailings with a telephone call or a personal visit.

THE BANQUET PROGRAM

Banquet business can prove tremendously lucrative for any restaurant. Their benefits are:

1. They offer profitable volume business for your restaurant.
2. They offer valuable publicity and good will generated among the individual banqueteers, prompting them to revisit your restaurant.
3. They offer referrals potential. The banquet attender "talks up" his meal and the restaurant facilities. It is estimated that each satisfied banqueteer tells an average of three other people about the banquet. This means an average of three word-of-mouth referrals for each satisfied banqueteer. This is extremely valuable, localized public relations that is worth a great deal in future guest flow.

DIRECT MAIL FOR BANQUET SALES

The mailing packages should contain the following elements:

1. *A sales letter.* This should be tailored to the particular market group you are trying to reach. In other words, a church group requires one letter, a business group a different one, and so on. You cannot depend on a single "catch-all" letter to motivate all groups. Strive to develop a close appeal for each recipient.
2. *A reply card* for prospects to indicate their interest, or to request a personal call or visit.

It is not necessary to send individually addressed letters when sending out mailings; organization names and the title of the prospect are usually sufficient. For example:

> Sales Manager
> XYZ Company
> Ann Arbor, Michigan

However, whenever you know the name of an executive who heads a prospective banquet organization, then you should direct a personalized letter to his or her attention:

> Ms. Roberta Johnson
> Vice President
> XYZ Co.
> Ann Arbor, Mich.

GUEST REFERRALS

Many restaurants obtain advance banquet information from guests who are members of a prospective banquet group. (It's surprising how many such leads are either volunteered or else obtained during the course of casual conversation.) In other instances, restaurants have placed printed notices in rooms, stating:

> "Do you belong to an organization planning a Banquet? We'd appreciate knowing about it.
> Listed below are just a few of the services we offer for your Banquet: (List of services follows.) Also included is a coupon for guests to fill out. Please leave it in the room or at the desk with the prospective banquet organization name, scheduled date, and who to contact."

PROCEDURES TO FOLLOW IN OBTAINING BANQUET BUSINESS FOR YOUR RESTAURANT

Below are listed procedures that will help you to organize and systematize your efforts in obtaining banquet business:

1. Compile name lists. Transcribe names pertaining to forthcoming banquets *in your area* on 3 × 5 index cards, inserting pertinent comments as to your contacts and results. Information should include: name and address of the organization, projected banquet date, name of the secretary or executive officer to contact. These cards are first placed in

an alphabetical file, and thereafter (subsequent to your contacting them) in a numerical file for automatic follow-up reference.

2. *Direct Mail Contact.* Your mailing to these groups should, ideally, comprise the following:

- An explanatory letter
- A descriptive brochure of your restaurant
- A return postcard (including an invitation to the secretary to have lunch or cocktails at your restaurant as your guest when visiting your city).

3. *Phone Contacts.* Such personalized approaches frequently produce desirable results. Follow up your telephone discussion with your brochure and an accompanying letter. An example of a possible telephone talk is contained below.

Suggested Contact Procedures

A regular, scheduled time for making telephone solicitations calls should be set up (a minimum of 3 hours each week). Each call should be followed up with a memo, a letter, or some other written reminder. This written message should include your banquet facilities, and whether you have previously sent out a brochure or not. After making your call, add any information or facts you have gained from the call on the contact file card with the contact's name or company.

Sample Telephone Solicitation

"It has come to our attention that you are planning a banquet (sales meeting, etc.) in our area in the near future. Knowing that you seek the *best* accommodations and the *best* specialized banquet facilities, we would like to recommend our restaurant for this event.

"We are experienced in accommodating banquets—both large and small. Among our guests have been such well-known organizations as:

(Give brief list of outstanding names of banquets that have appeared at your restaurant.)

Dear Mr. _____ :

Our restaurant takes special
pride in offering its delightful private dining facilities
for the use of the city's outstanding business firms, which
use our facilities for sales
dinner meetings, seminars, and
conferences. We also have special equipment available for
presentations, including slide
and movie projectors, sound
systems, chalkboards, etc.

Sales meetings are particularly
successful when conducted
after an expansive and bounti-
ful dinner at our restaurant.
Our spacious and unusual atmosphere creates a highly congenial
mood on the part of the diner,
which makes him receptive to a
dramatically presented program.

Please examine the enclosed literature detailing the facilities
of our dining palace, and feel
free to call me for additional
information. I shall be delighted to make a reservation for
your organization.

                    Cordially yours,

Dear Sir:

Our restaurant features the penultimate in dining pleasure, with the most extraordinary cuisine. It provides a delightful, plush, exciting emporium, with six separate, magnificent dining rooms, and a cocktail lounge. It also offers unusual and sophisticated entertainment suitable for the entire family.

Our restaurant takes special pride in offering private banquet facilities to the River City Organizations for their use in adding pleasure to the lives of the elderly. Special rates can be arranged for worthwhile causes, to help organizations raise much needed funds to continue their vitally important purposes.

Please examine the enlosed literature, detailing the facilities of our dining palace, and feel free to contact me for additional information. I shall be delighted to reserve our facilities for any function of yours. We have dates available starting in September, 1976.

Cordially yours,

"To be more specific, Mr. X, here are some of the highlights of our facilities: A fine dining room with plenty of room—50 people at a time can be accommodated. We also have a renowned cuisine in a variety of menus for your selection, a spacious meeting room, a speaker's platform, and speaking facilities.

"Our descriptive brochure—previously sent to you—points out many other features and specialized banquet services. In addition, we will be glad to provide specialized facilities to meet *your* banquet needs.

"Is there any other information we can supply you? May I set up an appointment at this time to meet with you and your banquet arrangment representatives to show them through our restaurant and help to correlate your banquet arrangements and activities?"

HOW TO ACCOMMODATE YOUR BANQUET GUESTS

Personalized Tie-Ins That Help Get Repeat Banquet Business

People and organizations like to feel that they are getting special, personal service. They also appreciate individual attention—for themselves as individuals, or for their organization as a whole. Catering to this desire can attract business to your restaurant and can assure repeat business. Among such services that have been effective in the past are the following, any one or combination of which can help your banquet business:

- Give special attention to decorating the banquet area in honor of the banquet being held.
- Arrange for a series of publicity stories about the banquet and submit them to local newspapers.
- Arrange for a local photographer to take pictures of the banquet and of individuals attending. It pays off.
- Showmanship also helps. One restaurant that accommodated a petroleum banquet dressed the bellboys in gas station attendant uniforms to greet the guests.

Chapter 13

Catering

CATERING: WHAT DOES IT MEAN TO YOU?

Catering used to mean all things for all occasions. The food, the china, the strolling violinist, the flowers, the waiters and waitresses, the hall: All could be supplied by or through the same source for a private, prearranged meal. This meal would be served to a party larger than restaurants usually accommodate. Although the menu might offer a choice of foods, no individual orders were taken. Today, however, *catering* can mean anything more elaborate than a take-out order for five tuna-fish-on-ryes.

If you establish a catering service, you'll want to consider whether to cater on premises or off, or both. You'll also have to decide how much advance notice you'll need for a catered meal and the maximum size of the party you can serve. And it will be your choice whether to supply waiters as well.

You'll need to answer all these questions before beginning a promotion campaign. But you still have to determine who your potential clients will be. Here are some possible markets. Look at the institutions in your area (and their present caterers) for others.

• Family and personal events: weddings, engagements, birthdays, anniversaries, holidays.

• Business conferences, luncheons, cocktail parties, press conferences for new products, Christmas parties. Meetings exclusively for executives are served a different menu from employees further down the totem pole.

• Industrywide associations and professional groups have become increasingly important as the demand for self- and government regulation has mounted along with the continual need of members to make contacts. They may meet in small policy-making groups or at the all-important annual convention. While you might not be able to get a crack at the main event of a convention, these annual conventions always spur unofficial parties and unpublicized meetings that aren't on the agenda.

• Educational institutions, from class graduations and trips to administrative meetings.

• Philanthropic organizations may hold their planning sessions or fund-raising appeals through a dinner honoring important contributors. Similarly, the organization may hold a breakfast for a particular segment of the working community or a cocktail party to attract new contributors who want a little fun for their donation.

• Athletic organizations, whether amateur or professional, celebrate games won or lost, tournaments, personalities, and the heroes of the season.

• Watch civic and political organizations. They often grow in leaps and bounds. A struggling environmental group that can barely afford a beer party today can become quite influential in the future. Or a wealthy member might throw a fancy bash to raise funds for an important community issue. This means publicity—possibly free publicity for you as a caterer. Be ready with imaginative ideas to charm the press.

• Religious institutions and organizations are not only centers of information for their congregation or their members, but also sponsors of fund-raising and social events.

• Hobby, recreational, and self-improvement organizations, and bridge, chess, and backgammon clubs often hold year-end dinners for their members. Similarly, people who have lost weight, overcome their fear of flying, or stopped smoking all have a very big occasion to celebrate.

• Tour groups.

● Children are a category unto themselves. Their idea of party foods is different from that of adults, both in food and party accessories.

● Off-premises retail outlets can be extremely lucrative, if planned well. Try to sell the best-known items on your menu through speciality food stores. And don't overlook department stores, which are more and more often catering to their customers' appetites. Henri Bendel, for example, one of New York City's most exclusive high-fashion department stores near Central Park, started an extremely successful food department that takes advantage of its location and proximity to the park. Take-out foods are sold as picnic lunches. The lunches use fresh foods that are prepared by a well-known gourmet shop. There is certainly no reason why an established restaurant could not take on a similar concession.

Once your retail outlets are established, they can be publicized by placing small cards on the tables of your restaurant advertising this feature. You could also include miscellaneous information on any food or tradition that is unusual. You should also indicate that customers can place advance orders at the retail outlet, but that these orders will be prepared in your own kitchen.

● Food in a new public area. If you're starting an outdoor cafe or food stand in a public area that has never had a food operation nearby, send a release to newspapers. Since you will have to work with local government to open a new place, you can emphasize the civic end of your work. Newspapers leap at upbeat civic stories.

● Food stands for special events such as country fairs or city block parties are excellent markets. New York City even had an outdoor event devoted to showing off the specialties of some of its best restaurants. Such stands can be expanded and converted into an informal outdoor restaurant in good weather by adding tables with festive umbrellas. Your town might even have a plaza or some other open space where you can buy a franchise.

HELPING YOU OVERCOME SLOW PERIODS

Catering can be vital to your financial stability in slow periods. But unless your competition is nil, that guarantee of future business takes long-range planning and promotion.

Mama Leone, for example, is a large, popular-priced restaurant in New York City's theater district that caters only on premises. Yet it has bookings as far as a year in advance. How does Mama Leone's compete? First, it obtains lists from the New York Convention Bureau. It sends three different form letters to groups throughout the country. Each letter mentions the restaurant's seating capacity and describes the eleven dining areas. Along with the letter is enclosed a choice of menus, with prices, including tips and taxes.

The restaurant attracts a wide spectrum of groups, from participants of a national electronics convention to members of athletic organizations, religious fund-raising groups, high school graduation classes, and theater parties. When such groups make a booking, they are asked general questions about their visit: why they have come to New York, what other activities they plan. A short release is then sent to the local paper where the group originates for an item on the social page. A steady stream of publicity-rich news is also fed to widely read gossip columnists.

USE PUBLIC RELATIONS LISTS

The New York Convention Bureau's weekly list of visitors to the city and contacts has its equivalent in other localities. These contacts are the first stage of your promotion campaign. You will need form letters to cope with large mailings. Such letters may read something like the ones on the following page.

Similar letters can be developed for tour groups, students, or any other organization that may be visiting your city or town. Make the letters as general as possible so they have broad appeal. Briefly mention the number of possible accommodations, food specialties ("We have been serving our Polynesian barbecue at private parties for ten years"), and your skill and experience. If you're either in a midtown location or in the immediate vicinity of the group's headquarters, this is also important for the group to know and certainly worth a postscript.

OFF-PREMISES CATERING

Most restaurants limit their catering to the restaurant itself. But the reverse is also common; some restaurants have too limited a seat-

Dear _____ :

We are delighted that you have selected our city as the site of your coming convention.

In scheduling events during the convention, may we suggest (name of restaurant) for private parties and meetings. Our four semi-private dining areas can hold from eight to two-hundred people, depending on the nature of the event. If a member of your organization will be coming here to survey possible locations for your program, we would be pleased to show him or her our facilities, which have served business clientele for 15 years. A brochure and sample menus with approximate prices are enclosed.

We look forward to the privilege of assisting in making your convention a wholly satisfying one. Please call for further information.

                Sincerely yours,

Letter to the parents of the bride:

Dear Mr. and Mrs. _____:

Congratulations on the happy news of your daughter's betrothal. You must be very proud.

Weddings are a very busy time for those who must make all of the many arrangements, and somehow they seem to multiply as they get closer to the big day. If you have already been through the experience, you know.

In this regard, I would like to point out that our restaurant not only has excellent dining facilities for any and all of your wedding requirements, but it also has a staff that is trained and experienced in all the things it takes to make a wedding a happy and memorable occasion.

Whether you have in mind a shower, a banquet, a wedding reception, a dinner, or simply guest accommodations, you may be sure that we will gladly assist you in every way to make things go smoothly.

You may very well wish to inspect our facilities in advance. If you do, kindly call me so that I may personally escort you and answer your questions.

Sincerely yours,

ANNOUNCING: In-Company Catering

The same famed, exciting food that's available at our restaurant can be brought to your conference rooms each day. At the exact time you say, delivered deliciously hot, ready to enjoy.

And it comes with all the trimmings--hot potato salad, cole slaw, pickles, and even a "tasting" of our famous chopped liver.

It's a BANQUET AT YOUR DESK. We cater to any and all company events, including:
- executive meetings
- sales conferences
- departmental sessions
- in-company seminars
- whatever!

Our meals will help make each meeting an EVENT and a spectacular success.

Enclosed is a copy of our menu and a list of companies to whom we now cater in-company meals. May we include your company in this list?

We're as close to you as your phone. Phone today, while this message is still fresh in your mind.

Cordially,

ing capacity to cater on premises, but can capitalize on their reputation by catering off premises. If this is the case, however, such service is not likely to include waiters or any further service beyond food. *Fine and Shapiro,* a restaurant with a very popular home catering service, specializes in cold buffets, but also prepares for small dinner parties. Anything more than this they found a drain on the restaurant itself.

Catering service is becoming increasingly important to restaurateurs. Many quality restaurants that did not have catering service before promote it now. *The Cattleman* in New York City has given their catering service—which is basically a take-out service—a special telephone number and name, "Dial-A-Steak." The service is advertised in publications likely to be read by business and professional executives who are likely customers for dinner meetings. Up to 15 dinners at a time can be ordered through Dial-A-Steak. The Cattleman also throws in a surprise gift with orders, such as a Cattleman cookbook.

There are many food ideas that can be adapted to quality menus in which the food will not be damaged in transit and does not need to be heated at its destination. Cold salads are a superb catering offering, and their variety is endless.

Another way to make a hit is by catering exclusively diet lunches. Most take-out lunches are saturated with starch. Often salads are dull and/or lack crispness, and their dressings are full of mayonnaise. There's a lot of room for improvement in this area, as well as a heavy demand for quality foods.

Restaurants that have tried this variation have called it "Dial-a-Diet-Lunch," or "The Dieter's Lunch." If you want to try it, distribute flyers on the streets of your business area. One restaurant that offers "The Nickolaus Diet Lunch" has a flyer of postcard size that shows four women picnicking outside an office building. "Gina, Sylvia, Linda, and Dell have lost weight," the copy reads, "with The Nickolaus Diet Lunch." Inside are quotes from a news program with quotes from satisfied customers. Below that are five days of imaginative menus. On the back is the cost.

Lunches can be ordered individually. But by joining a Lunch Club, the dieters commit themselves to a month or a week of Nickolaus meals. The longer the commitment, the lower the price, which is even at its most expensive moderate. Another favorable news story is quoted next to the details of the lunch plan.

BROCHURES

Many restaurants and catering firms claim to rely on word of mouth for business. But even here, there must be a bare minimum of advertising: listings in the yellow pages and an ad in the annual banqueting sections of regional newspapers.

A brochure and perhaps a short announcement on your menu that you hold private parties are both important ways to convey information about your catering possibilities. A brochure that's heavy on atmosphere and light on details about prices, which change, can offer significant savings. However, you should include a description of the rooms and the number of people that can be served in each.

The less specific, the less frequently the format must be changed. You can therefore afford to invest in four-color artwork, and a more visually dramatic brochure.

The Atmosphere Brochure

A brochure for the *Blackhawk* announces:

"Accommodations for private parties, 25 to 250. The Executive Suite has two elegantly paneled rooms for luncheons and dinners." (One of the rooms is sketched on the brochure.)

"The Frontier Room with its Red Dog Palace Saloon for informal hospitality buffet service is available.

"A tape recorder, P/A system, piano, dance floor, and entertainment arrangements are available."

This is the atmospheric approach.

The design and layout in Blackhawk's brochure are almost as important as the words themselves. They convey the same feeling and atmosphere that the restaurant offers. The brochure gives little space to food, except for a passing reference to roast beef, steaks, and salads. If a reader has any further questions he is referred to the catering department.

In this type of brochure, all the specifics can be summed up in a generalization. A San Francisco steak house brochure, for example, says:

"It's easy to plan at (name of restaurant). You select from any

CATERING

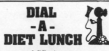

Nickolaus Diet Lunch Club in New York delivers to offices. Orders must be placed one day in advance.

Junior's in New York specializes in catering for every occasion— promoting their services with this menu.

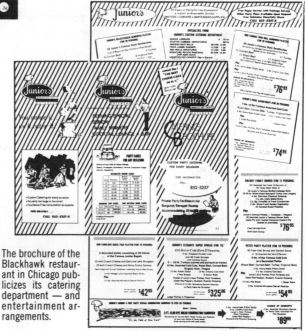

The brochure of the Blackhawk restaurant in Chicago publicizes its catering department — and entertainment arrangements.

of several menu suggestions . . . or make up your own from our large menu! The cost is less than you think. Group dinners can be arranged at very reasonable costs, served with fine taste and distinctive flair."

Junior's, a very popular, unpretentious, family-oriented restaurant in New York City, puts out an entirely different brochure—very unlike Blackhawk's.

Junior's menu takes a family-oriented approach rather than an executive suite approach. In addition, the exterior of the brochure is jammed with information offering free consultations for occasions of any size, listing menus for two elaborate catered dinners, and prices for special occasion cakes.

Inside, the foldout describes no less than 11 catered menus. It lists each item, the amount of food by weight (turkey in raw weight), and the prices. Catering specialties not on the menus are also listed within, with prices by the pound or gallon. Barely visible is a note at the top of the page noting that serving equipment, paper service, or help is available and can be rented, bought, or hired from the restaurant. This is a rarity in running either a full-scale catering service or a busy restaurant.

In summation, the menu comprises your "catalogue" of the products (and services) you have to offer. It also depicts your own personal image and style. Plan for the future in the preparation of your menu, avoid constant changes that can prove expensive.

Chapter 14

31 Ways to a More Effective Operation

If you have studied the ideas in the previous chapters, you should be well on your way to improving your image and upgrading your operations.

This chapter has 31 more ideas to offer you that will help you build a more effective operation. Study these ideas. Apply them to your own operation. They can make the difference between repeat vs. one-time business. If you use these ideas wisely, they will make people want to do business with you and you only.

1. *Remember names and places.* Ever meet a business acquaintance after a long time of separation? He smiled, grabbed you by the hand, and greeted you by name. Weren't you flattered? On the other hand, if he had forgotten your name, you might not have felt very good. Remembering names is good for your image. Try to develop the habit; it will pay dividends.

2. *Be a joiner.* Socializing, mixing, and mingling with people can be fun. It gets you out of yourself. It broadens you. More important, it is good business. Joining clubs and organizations not only allows you to help others, but it also puts you in contact with people

who can help you and your business. The contacts you make can be useful.

3. *Be a good listener*. We all enjoy talking about ourselves, and we are often partial toward those who enjoy listening to what we have to say. If you listen, you'll get to know people better. You'll know more about them. It is your way of showing your interest in them. People who feel cared about and liked will always come back.

4. *Play up the YOU appeal*. Make the customer feel important, a distinguished personage; show that you cherish his patronage. Strive to convey this feeling, and he will feel similarly about you and your restaurant.

5. *Be helpful*. Assist in various, spontaneous ways. For example, make meal suggestions or show an interest in how he enjoyed the meal. There are literally hundreds of ways to demonstrate your interest in his welfare.

6. *Demonstrate your integrity*. Let people know that you keep your word. Live up to the promises you make. This is particularly pertinent to scheduled group business, involving a multitude of details and contractual commitments. Integrity is also reflected in the consistent quality of your products and service. The public is not inclined to tolerate poor quality food or unpleasant surroundings. Customers want more than just food from their restaurants. Integrity and personal interest are important qualities to have. Your reputation will spread quickly among the public through word of mouth and will pay off in business referrals.

7. *Be consistent*. Strive to avoid unpleasant "surprises." Maintain consistently good quality and service and careful attention to your individual guests. I know one restaurateur who gave three different banquet customers three different prices for the menus during a one-month period. Unfortunately, these customers were members of the same women's club. They compared notes, and he lost all three as customers. Such inconsistencies cause serious damage to your image. If your prices need adjustment, do so and strive to keep the prices stable for at least six months.

8. *Give all customers special attention*. Special attention and personal interest is always appreciated. This extra interest will pay off in additional business. Take the case of Frank Murphy, a small chain franchisee I know. He turned a disaster into a triumph. One day, just by accident, he stopped at a table where a woman had purchased a

veal cutlet parmagiana. He was shocked when his friendly inquiries about the meal met with a storm of abuse. The sauce was too spicy, and the cheese was burned. Frank took it back and gave her another selection. The service he performed for this customer made her a permanent friend of the restaurant and brought him several new customers by referral.

9. *Be creative.* You can show your creativity in many ways. One restaurateur, for example, had an artist sketch a complimentary picture of new guests. Another restaurant provided amusements for children, keeping them busy while the parents awaited their meal. A Michigan restaurant kept careful records of each customer's favorite dishes, drinks, etc., enabling him to provide personalized service.

10. *Be systematic.* Organization and planning can make things easier for you. The old exhortation, "Plan your day and work your plan" is more true today than ever. Many restaurants have a prepared check list of daily "Things To Do"; also Operations Manuals, to help formalize their procedures and enabling better delegation.

11. *Be self-motivating.* Business is a constant school of hard knocks. So many things can go wrong. Don't let adversity wrestle you to the mat. Take a positive attitude toward it. Remember the sun shines most brilliantly after a heavy shower. I remember a restaurant owner who had the largest party order in his history. Suddenly his meat supplier had a strike and couldn't deliver. The owner was fit to be tied. He was very depressed, but then his natural bounce asserted itself. He went out and found another supplier. And to top it off, his new source sold him the product for less than the old one. View setbacks in their proper perspective and set your business course with conviction and determination.

12. *Be affirmative, not negative.* Nobody likes a complainer. There's no sound reason for it. Stressing the deficiencies of a rival operation invites suspicion. When someone knocks a competitive restaurant —even though what he says is true—there's a tendency for the customer to attribute the remarks to "sour grapes" rather than believing them. Instead, emphasize what you and your restaurant do. People will like you better for it.

13. *Be thoughtful and considerate.* A friendly relationship with your customers will take you a long way. The best way to do this is through a genuine interest in them. A follow-up thank you note as a birthday card can create good will. At little cost in money or time, it

broadens your base of communication. Thoughtfulness of this kind will not only give you personal satisfaction, but also brings in dividends.

14. *Be alert.* Watch for new ideas and developments in your area. Read the major business publications and the trade press. Find out what your competitors are doing. Think about how to improve your food and services by incorporating a new material, a new way of doing things, a new process. Most of all see how these ideas can be turned to the advantage of your customer.

15. *Present a neat appearance.* A businessman makes his best impression when he's dressed in a fairly conventional manner. Sporting expensive-type jewelry, racetrack-type neckwear, or sports shirts can turn customers off. Customers like to deal with people who take themselves seriously.

Pay attention to the details of your daily dress. Avoid the tie that is ever-so-lightly stained, the suit that is losing its press. The same is true of the dishes you offer. Nothing can be more harmful or discouraging to sales than brown lettuce or lumpy mashed potatoes.

16. *Be patient.* Remember that potential customers don't know your restaurant or service as well as you do. What you may consider basic logic may not appear so to your customers. If there are extra-long waits for certain dishes, tell them, and explain the reasons why.

Also be patient with people who work for you. Often employees need a little careful cultivation to turn out well. And finally, be patient with yourself. Don't be your own severest critic.

17. *Be authoritative.* You must be the expert, displaying the expertise needed to carry the day. You must read up on new restaurant programs and offerings, and familiarize yourself thoroughly with alternative products and offerings. In this way you can give the customer the very best possible products and services, so your customers can depend on you and give you their respect and loyalty.

18. *Show deference.* Though you should always maintain your aura of expertise, there will be times when your customer also regards himself as an "expert" in judging and commenting on the quality of your food and service, sometimes negatively. Don't scoff, even if you disagree. Being deferential on such occasions may lose the debate, but it can win the customer's good will and return patronage.

19. *Be generous.* Have the customers complained? Follow the credo that the customer is always right, even if you don't believe he is. Better allow yourself to be "taken advantage of" in some instances

than to win the argument and lose the customer. In such instances, the most important casualty is your image.

20. *Be punctual.* This is particularly applicable to group dinner arrangements, banquet schedules, etc. It is also applicable to your day-by-day service. Nothing loses customers more frequently than "lagging service." If you take reservations, keep them close to the appointed time. Remember that time is money. Lack of punctuality may be regarded as an insult by your customer and an indication that you consider your time worth more than his. It is also considered a sign that you do not take your business reservations seriously.

21. *Display good manners.* This may seem elementary, yet it is of vital importance in building a good image. Little things like apologizing for unexpectedly long waits or for running out of special dishes make a big difference. They help establish your restaurant as a place where it is nice to do business.

22. *Be original.* Don't allow yourself to become dull or monotonous with the same unchanged dishes and approaches. If you serve the same dishes all year round, boredom sets in quickly, not only for your customer, but for you, too. Constantly analyze your operation. Seek to dramatize and to give excitement to your dishes. Try to dramatize the preparation and appearance of your food. It creates new interest in your operation.

23. *Be cheerful.* Maintain a cheery demeanor. Make every effort to keep your personal troubles out of your business life. Dejection communicates itself and dampens both your sales efforts and your customers' interest. A ready, sincere smile is a good way to impress others with your desire to be friendly and accommodating. Good cheer has a way of spreading itself to others. It is infectious and reciprocal, and encourages people to want to be in your atmosphere and among cheerful people.

24. *Be an anticipator.* An effective restaurateur tries to anticipate the personal factors, the problems, the questions that may arise. Try to see what you can find out about the nature of your market. Is your typical customer the friendly, informal type who likes to chat with the owner? Is he the authoritative type who expects deference and formality from restaurant employees? Is he a businesslike person who wants to get to the meal quickly? This kind of forethought will permit you to run your operation according to the desires of the greatest number of customers.

25. *Keep files.* For those of us who haven't total recall, keeping

files on your best customers provides an invaluable record which can be referred to in the future. It should include all the key points and dates you should remember. You can see what satisfied or didn't. You can prepare yourself for the expectations and attitudes of your best customers. Although this does involve additional time and effort, your work will be well-rewarded in customer loyalty and satisfaction.

26. *Be friendly, but not overly familiar.* There is a fine line between friendship and overfamiliarity. You need to be able to sense when you are overstepping it. So often it will depend on the nature of the customer you are dealing with. What will be acceptable to one will be annoying to the other. When in doubt, fall back to a less familiar, more formal position. Try to remember that a customer may feel pressured by overfamiliarity. On the other hand, never back off when your customer clearly seeks a more personal relationship.

27. *Get fun out of your work.* Always show that you enjoy your work and your customers. The attitude becomes contagious; the customer will reciprocate by enjoying your restaurant and you. Display a grouchy demeanour and watch how quickly your patronage evaporates. If your work is a deadly bore to you, you'll certainly fail at it. It won't be something you don't want to do, but rather, feel you ought to do, something that you have to push yourself to do each day. If you want your customers to enjoy eating at your restaurant rather than at your competitor's, you should enjoy your work.

28. *Display self-respect.* Be respectful to your customers, but also respectful to yourself. Maintain your own dignity and status. If you wish your customer to respect you, you must respect yourself. Be polite but not servile. In this day and age, servility is not considered a virtue.

29. *Be forthright.* Answer all questions fully and fairly—right on the line. Don't give inadequate half-answers. When your prospect realizes you are not trying to duck or to evade issues, he will respect you, and that respect will be communicated to your product or service.

30. *Exercise polite persistence.* A turn-down is no reason to be deterred from trying again. After a reasonable waiting period, you are free to make a polite renewal of your sales effort. It won't offend the customer, and may well bring about a sale. Once again, it becomes a matter of being able to know when persistence becomes offensive because of ill-timed insistence, and when it is merited.

31. *Be honest in your claims.* In your advertising claims, don't overwhelm the customer with exaggerations or extravagant claims.

This only results in disappointed customers. Stick to the facts and make sure they are well understood. If you do this, you'll be doing all you can to encourage customers and to maintain good will.

By this time, you have become aware of what goes into creating an image. As you see, you are the artist who paints his own picture. The manner in which you handle yourself, the impression you give, the integrity, consistency, sincerity, and planning you display are the main brush strokes on the canvas. They provide the reasons why people will want to do business with you and you alone. They are your image and the key to your success.

The important thing to remember is that each of your customers is a personal, important individual. Your objective is to build an image which caters to him individually; one that is so positively radiant that it sets you apart from your competitors. Undoubtedly you are already doing some things that are right. Now go ahead and add to them. Good luck!

Index